I0540204

Toward a Materialist Conception
of Music History

Historical Materialism Book Series

The Historical Materialism Book Series is a major publishing initiative of the radical left. The capitalist crisis of the twenty-first century has been met by a resurgence of interest in critical Marxist theory. At the same time, the publishing institutions committed to Marxism have contracted markedly since the high point of the 1970s. The Historical Materialism Book Series is dedicated to addressing this situation by making available important works of Marxist theory. The aim of the series is to publish important theoretical contributions as the basis for vigorous intellectual debate and exchange on the left.

The peer-reviewed series publishes original monographs, translated texts, and reprints of classics across the bounds of academic disciplinary agendas and across the divisions of the left. The series is particularly concerned to encourage the internationalization of Marxist debate and aims to translate significant studies from beyond the English-speaking world.

For a full list of titles in the Historical Materialism Book Series available in paperback from Haymarket Books, visit: www.haymarketbooks.org/series_collections/1-historical-materialism.

Toward a Materialist Conception of Music History

Stephan Hammel

Haymarket Books
Chicago, IL

First published in 2024 by Brill Academic Publishers, The Netherlands
© 2024 Koninklijke Brill NV, Leiden, The Netherlands

Published in paperback in 2025 by
Haymarket Books
P.O. Box 180165
Chicago, IL 60618
773-583-7884
www.haymarketbooks.org

ISBN: 979-8-88890-542-5

Distributed to the trade in the US through Consortium Book Sales and
Distribution (www.cbsd.com) and internationally through Ingram
Publisher Services International (www.ingramcontent.com).

This book was published with the generous support of Lannan
Foundation, Wallace Action Fund, and the Marguerite Casey Foundation.

Special discounts are available for bulk purchases by organizations and
institutions. Please call 773-583-7884 or email info@haymarketbooks.org
for more information.

Cover art and design by David Mabb. Cover art is a development of
*Painting 41, Rhythm 69 (William Morris Block Printed Pattern Book, with
a Hans Richter Storyboard, developed from Richter's* Rhythmus 25 *and
Kazimir Malevich's film script* Artistic and Scientific Film – Painting and
Architectural Concerns – Approaching the New Plastic Architectural
System*).* Paint and wallpaper on canvas (2007).

Printed in the United States.

Library of Congress Cataloging-in-Publication data is available.

Contents

Acknowledgements

I came to the positions I take in this book by way of countless arguments and exchanges with comrades and colleagues. These friends allowed me to vociferously defend only mildly plausible views while I was finding my way to better ones, most often with their help. I am deeply grateful to my colleague Amy Bauer, who read and commented on every chapter as it was being drafted. Her unflagging seriousness about ideas, and her insistence on clarity and concreteness, were invaluable to me. At UC Irvine, I also enjoyed guidance and support from David Brodbeck, Colleen Reardon, and Nicole Grimes.

Standing as it does somewhat outside the academic mainstream, Marxism is an intellectual tradition most often inherited in the context of political organising. I am exceedingly fortunate that my activities on the organised Left led me to Kevin Anderson and Peter Hudis. Their deep knowledge about Marxism's philosophical foundations continues to shape my approach to the field. The whole time I was working on this project, I was also reading, studying, and debating with Nathan Fisher, Matthew Taylor, and Jason Netek. These comrades remain my role models in intellectual self-development.

The inspiration for this project sprang from my work with Bryan Parkhurst. I count the time I spent writing and thinking with him as among the most important intellectual experiences of my life. This book would certainly never have been written without him.

I am terribly grateful to my parents whose unflagging faith in me has kept me afloat all these years. I cherish their love and wisdom.

Much of this text was written during pandemic quarantine. Brandon Gremchuck's help, patience, and perspective in those long months made it possible for me to live well while I worked. He remains a model friend.

Introduction

On the 10th of November 1938 officers arrived at Guido Adler's villa in a Vienna suburb to search his home for Jewish residents. The renowned founder of *Musikwissenschaft* was in his eighty-fourth year and suffering from dementia. His daughter Melanie resided with him and, with the help of a housekeeper, provided care for her father. Adler's research and editorial activities had long ceased. A faithful former student, Carl Rosenthal, had taken over control of his library, correspondence and what was left of his duties.[1] Among the projects that Adler left incomplete at the time of his mandated retirement from the University of Vienna was the publication series *Denkmäler der Tonkunst in Österreich* [Monuments of Tonal Art in Austria], which had begun to appear in 1892, when Adler was in his early thirties. The archives associated with the project had been housed at the university; however, soon after 1927 they were removed and, sometime around 1930, relocated to Adler's home. Four decades old, the *Denkmäler* project was stalled, but not forgotten. Accompanying the officers that day was another former Adler student, Alfred Orel, an expert on fifteenth-century counterpoint and a longtime fascist activist. He took possession of the archive. Rosenthal and the Adlers were all of Jewish descent, but none were arrested that day. Rosenthal and Adler's son, Hubert Joachim, eventually settled in the United States. Guido Alder and his daughter remained in Vienna.

It is unclear how Adler managed to avoid deportation. It is suggested by Rosenthal and others that his age, declining health, and scholarly fame protected him. Indeed, he continued to receive his university pension until his death. It should be noted, however, that Austrian Jewish intellectuals were far from immune to right-wing persecution in this period. The philologist Elise Richter, only ten years Adler's junior and the first woman to hold an academic appointment at the University of Vienna perished at Theresienstadt in 1943. Melanie Adler was arrested months after her father's death and was murdered at an extermination camp in 1944.

Orel's confiscation of the *Denkmäler* archive marks a decisive end to musicology's early liberal phase. Institutionalized by virtue of enlightened university reforms, the young science of music history could, for a time, exemplify progressive modernity without having to confront its inherent contradictions. Adler was himself a man of liberal convictions who could contribute as read-

---

1 Rosenthal 1985–86.

ily to the preservation of Catholic liturgy as he could to the defence of modern music. He was also able to resist an essentialist view of national identity, apparently absent any influence from socialist internationalism. At the time of his death, Adler was a political anachronism. If his life was spared, it is perhaps because he ultimately fell through the cracks of fascist ideology, and was consequently invisible. The political distance between Adler and Orel takes the measure of a gap in intellectual history. If we understand fascism to originate in reaction to revolutionary socialism – and to be ultimately unintelligible without it – then we can conclude that the intellectual history of the discipline missed a step, so to speak.[2] It is noteworthy that at the time the Hitler regime took over musicological research funding and publication functions in Germany, it did not have to contend with historical materialism in the discipline. In other fields, such as the historiography of the French Revolution, Marxism had earned lasting influence. Musicology, however, never engaged with historical materialism in a sustained manner, and cannot be said ever to have gone through a Marxist phrase.

By the end of the Second World War, the most propitious moments for a musicological encounter with Marxism were in the past. In the decades around the turn of the twentieth century, the two discourses had key features in common. Both were powerfully shaped by the legacy of German Idealism while rebuking metaphysics, and both aimed to be a science of history. However, the war's disruptions and displacements, combined with the onset of the Cold War, created conditions highly unfavourable to the appropriation of historical materialism by music historians outside the Soviet sphere. Indeed, the field fractured. Musicologists working in socialist states were little read in the West, and humanistic scholarship produced in states aligned with NATO was often explicitly anti-communist. As late as 1962, four years before his death, the composer Hanns Eisler could only look forward to a time when the academic study of music would come to adopt Marxist methodological foundations. Even while he implicitly admitted to Marxism's failure to make substantive contributions to music history, Eisler nonetheless confidently predicted that musicologists would eventually be compelled to dispense with any conception of 'the autonomous, abstract development of musical material', because 'music develops in class struggle, for class struggle is the source of all productivity'. Not only will 'the history of music [be] written by Marxists', he writes, but 'the music theory of our time ought to be a dialectical materialist theory'.[3]

---

2   For more on the relationship of fascism to revolutionary socialism, see Parenti 1997.

3   Eisler 1978, p. 197.

Eisler's predictions are bold, but hardly surprising. After all, those committed to scientific socialism have routinely indulged in optimistic predictions
about the eventual success of the intellectual project, as well as the fulfilment
of associated political aims, since the founding of the Second International
at the latest. In fact, Marxism's critics frequently cite the unfulfilled predictions of its adherents as evidence against the doctrine. Eisler's projections,
however, do appear to have fared better than one might expect, especially given
that the chief source of his optimism was the 'building up [of] our socialist production' in actually existing socialist states.[4] Beginning in the closing
years of the Cold War, English-speaking musicologists engaged in sustained
and successful efforts to introduce methodological pluralism into a field many
practitioners felt had been too long dominated by outmoded and blinkered
approaches. In the immediate wake of the fall of the Berlin Wall, the pathbreaking feminist musicologist Marcia Citron celebrated the turn, writing that
'music courses deploying interdisciplinary theoretical approaches, including
semiotics, deconstruction, Marxism, and psychoanalytic theory, are sprouting
up in PhD programs, and their seeds are fertilising discourse throughout the
profession, in the form of provocative papers, journal articles, and even books'.[5]
The inclusion of Marxism in this list of theoretical strains newly welcome in
musicology is striking given that the return of Russia to the community of
capitalist states appeared to most observers to signal the end of revolutionary communism, or, as one conservative philosopher all-too-famously put it,
'the end of history'. That said, socialism's apparent failure may have so thoroughly disarticulated Marxism from its political content in the minds of most
American academics that its use in musicological research could appear harm-
less.

The kind of Marxism that has so far proven itself amenable to musicological use largely bypasses the tradition Eisler would have recognized as his own.
Eisler's political commitments developed in the wake of the 1917 Bolshevik
revolution, and the splintering of the German Social Democratic Party (SPD)
over the question of party support for war. Both of Eisler's elder siblings were
prominent in the left wing of the socialist movement. Ruth Fischer, his sister,
was among the very first members of the Austrian Communist Party (KPÖ) at
the time it was founded in 1918. She would eventually come into leadership in
the German Communist Party (KPD) after the failure of the March Action in
1921, insisting on a hard line against collaboration with the social democratic

---

4 Eisler 1978, p. 201.
5 Citron 1990, p. 115.

right. Gerhart Eisler served as an editor for *Die Rote Fahne* in the 1920s and eventually took up a government post in East Germany after the Second World War. Hanns Eisler was never a politician himself, and for that reason his career was not directly shaped by the shifting priorities of the Comintern during the period of Stalin's consolidation of power. Nevertheless, his political orientation is not hard to discern. In 1931, he praised the advent of a 'revolutionary opposition' in the German Workers' Choral Society (DASB) to combat the conservatism of its leadership, a position consistent with the Comintern's opposition to making common cause with reformist socialism.[6] He advocated for an explicitly materialist approach to the study of music history, and gave a series of lectures on the topic in party schools for workers' education. Developing the approach was a historical imperative, as capitalist investment in theatrical and concert performances was chronically insufficient to guarantee productive employment for professional musicians. With the rapid dissolution of traditional forms of music patronage, the professional musician was increasingly forced to compete for work with amateurs. At the same time, millions of Germans joined thousands of choral societies and amateur orchestras throughout the country during the Weimar period. Picking up on this trend, working-class organisations formed their own ensembles. So rapid and impressive was the success of workers' choruses in Germany that the movement won the praise of Lenin in 1913. He wrote that:

> ... no amount of police harassment can prevent the singing of the hearty proletarian song about mankind's coming emancipation from wage-slavery in all the great cities of the world, in all the factory neighborhoods, and more and more frequently in the huts of village laborers.[7]

Social democratic strategy had long understood the political organs of the working class, in particular the strike committees, as the basis for workers' control of industry. The proletarian choral society, Eisler thought, could play a similar role in organising a post-capitalist music making system. His vision for musical life under socialism was radically participatory, a feature that would allow the distinction of musician and auditor to wither away. In his words:

> The concert form arose in the epoch of the bourgeoisie and is useless for the purposes of the revolutionary working class. It can only offer noncom-

---

6   The details of Eisler's political life can be read in Betz 1982.
7   Lenin 1971 [1913], p. 225.

mittal pleasure and make the listener passive. In the next few years it will be our task to develop further the ideas of the didactic play in practical experiment.[8]

The course of history, however, guaranteed that such experiments would not occur: two years after those sentences were written, the Nazis came to power.

Eisler's Marxism embraced a number of commitments largely eschewed by scholars in the humanities, including those who explicitly align themselves with the Left. He was an economic determinist, untroubled by the threat of 'vulgar Marxism', and accordingly focused on transforming relations of production in the music making system. He rejected eclecticism and valued orthodoxy as a sign of theoretical consistency. Notably, his theoretical contributions were intended to appeal not only to other intellectuals, but also to workers, whom he took to embody a progressive force in history. These features of his Marxism contrast markedly with a consensus among many Left scholars that sees in economic determinism a threat to the intelligibility of subjective agency. This consensus associates the principle of orthodoxy with an antiquated form of party loyalty, and understands the political potential of the working class to have long receded irrecoverably into the past. These views on orthodox Marxism's limitations were shaped by a series of critiques that were powerfully influential in the West during the Cold War. In Fredric Jameson's estimation, the most significant of these came from two distinct sources. The first was:

> ... a philosophical 'post-Marxism' dating from the late 1960s, in which an emergent new feminism joins forces with a variety of post-structuralisms in the stigmatisation of such classical Marxist themes as totality and totalisation, telos, the referent, production, and so forth.

The other was:

> ... an intellectual Right, slowly emerging in the course of the 1980s, which seizes on the dissolution of Eastern European communism to affirm the bankruptcy of socialism as such and the definitive primacy of the market.[9]

By the 1990s, Moishe Postone could refer to a 'crisis of traditional Marxism', and propose that only a wholesale reinterpretation of Marx's political eco-

---

8   Eisler 1978, p. 39.
9   Jameson 2009, p. 367.

nomic categories could preserve his theory from anachronism.[10] While 'traditional' Marxism sustained serious reputational damage, especially in the period immediately succeeding the collapse of the Soviet Union, its theoretical legacy could nonetheless be productively mined in the academy. If the concept of exploitation attracted ever less attention, the same cannot be said about such concepts as alienation, commodification, or fetishism. The power of these conceptions allowed a species of Marxism to persist, primarily in the work of humanists and cultural theorists.[11]

However, with the onset of the Great Recession following the financial collapse of 2008–9, the situation began to change. Any confidence that mainstream economics had supplied policy makers with the tools needed to mitigate capitalism's crisis tendencies could no longer be sustained. In fact, the failure of most in the field to predict the collapse served to discredit many mainstream economic doctrines. Heterodox political economy consequently received renewed attention in the academy and in the press. Books such as Terry Eagleton's *Why Marx Was Right* indicated the direction of the ideological winds.[12] Yannis Varoufakis, an economist who became well-known on the Left when he served as Greek finance minister in the Syriza government, began to openly refer to himself as an 'erratic Marxist'.[13] Meanwhile, much less erratic Marxists, including Andrew Kliman and Paul Mattick Jr., demonstrated the power of value theory to explain the historical shifts that were underway.[14] The new relevance of Marx's political economy was further registered by the appearance of numerous commentaries on *Capital*, as well as re-evaluations of once hopelessly arcane aspects of the theory of value.[15] In recent years, numerous studies and, especially, translations of classic texts from the past, have made it newly possible to meet the current moment by reconstructing and reinterpreting the Marxist theoretical legacy.[16] Such a reinterpretation is,

---

10   Postone 1993.

11   In music studies, this persistence can be seen in Attali 1985, p. 5: 'Fetishized as a commodity, music is illustrative of the evolution of our entire society: deritualize a social form, repress an activity of the body, specialize its practice, sell it as a spectacle, generalize its consumption, then see to it that it is stockpiled until it loses its meaning'. For a more recent example, see James 2010.

12   Eagleton 2011.

13   Varoufakos 2015.

14   Kliman 2011; Mattick 2011.

15   Harvey 2018; Heinrich 2012; Moseley 2017.

16   This literature is larger than the scope of a footnote will allow, but must, at the very least, include the work of Rick Kuhn, Ben Lewis, Daniel Gaido, and Richard Day, among others.

indeed, vital to the further development of socialism now that Leninism has ceased to be a living political tendency, and the intellectual habits of the Cold War have outlived their usefulness. Today, Marxism can be said to be enjoying a new moment, one that need not choose between party orthodoxy and cultural studies.

This book aims to make good on this new moment in Marxism by reposing the question of whether historical materialism can serve as methodological foundation for music history. The question has to be reposed, rather than simply answered, for a number of reasons. In the first place, Marxists today are not in agreement about the ultimate viability, or even desirability, of an economic interpretation of history. A set of influential historians including Robert Brenner and Ellen Meiksins Wood, often referred to as 'Political Marxists', has led the charge to abandon the traditional form of historical materialism based on Marx's outline in the 1859 *Preface to A Critique of Political Economy* in favour of a non-teleological theory of historical change. Their model presumes that relations of production can transform independently of productivity increases in the forces of production. Others have inherited the defence of the traditional doctrine from G.A. Cohen and others associated with 'Analytic Marxism'. This is characteristic of a younger generation of Marxists whose commitments were little influenced by either the Cold War or the New Left. However, even those predisposed to accept classical historical materialism might balk at the extension of its method to the history of the arts. While it has often been argued that scientific socialism represents the sublation of philosophy, most would not presume on that basis that a Marxist aesthetics is therefore a contradiction in terms. After all, there exists a substantial literature that understands itself as contributing to just such a discourse. In the context of contemporary Marxism, then, the question of a materialist conception of music history must first be motivated before it can be fully meaningful.

A similar effort to motivate the question is required in the context of contemporary musicology. It can be argued that the work of critical theorists, especially Theodor Adorno, has been so productive for the discipline that introducing another – perhaps even incompatible – Marxist framework into the field could only be wilful and superfluous. Further, it cannot be taken for granted that musicological discourse is amenable to historical materialism's elemental categories in the first place. In order to be genuinely compelling for the music historian of whatever political persuasion, it must be shown that there is, in fact, space and need for apparently abstract theories about the driving forces of history. A materialist conception of music history is only viable if it is responsive to concerns native to the discipline.

The studies collected below constitute a response to the challenges involved in coherently asking after a materialist conception of music history. While ultimately intended to clear the way for future research, what follows is not merely preliminary. Each chapter aims to make an independent contribution to either the Marxist literature on the arts, or the musicological debate about method, or both, as is the case in the final chapter. Readers outside the United States will doubtless note that my perspective is decidedly American. I can only say here that I came by this limitation honestly. However, given the fact that the American fraction of the discipline has exerted such widespread influence on the global field, it is possible that this perspective can still speak to a broad audience.

The Realist Conception of Art

Verzeiht uns Epigrammendingen,
Wenn wir fatale Weisen singen,
Wir haben uns nach Hegel einstudiert,
Auf sein' Ästhetik noch nicht – abgeführt.

· · ·

Forgive us our epigrams
As we sing unpleasant tunes
For by rote we have studied Hegel,
And we are not yet purged of his *Aesthetics*.

KARL MARX (1836)[1]

In the summer of 1934, tens of thousands of Soviet citizens gathered in a public park to attend the opening of the Congress of Soviet Writers. Over two
weeks, hundreds of delegates delivered speeches to those assembled on the
problems of revolutionary aesthetics, the current state of literary production,
and the immediate political tasks of Soviet poetry, among other topics. The
event marked the beginning of a new stage of socialist construction in the cultural sphere. The Congress culminated in the founding of the Union of Soviet
Writers, a body which supplanted the various writers' organisations that had
emerged since 1917, in particular those associated with the 'proletarian culture', or *Proletkult* movement. In this way, Soviet authors would work hand
in hand with the Party in accomplishing the many unfinished tasks of the
social revolution. Prominent figures attended the conference, including Maxim
Gorky, arguably the intellectual leader of the Congress, Nikolai Bukharin, and
Karl Radek. These were joined by writers sympathetic to the Soviet project from

---

1 For a discussion of Marx's long-neglected early poetry, see Johnston 1967.

outside the Union. Willi Brendel, Louis Aragon, and André Malraux gave speeches, while Romain Rolland, George Bernard Shaw, and Upton Sinclair sent messages of support. The clear and immediate threat of fascism in Europe gave those invested in Soviet development further impetus to solidarize with the party that had carried out the only successful proletarian political revolution in history.

Those who spoke at the Congress had come to a consensus about what the October Revolution meant for the arts. First and foremost, it meant that tendentiousness in support of socialism was no aesthetic vice. Further, because Soviet democracy represented a new stage in social evolution, it is intuitive that this should also correspond to a transformation in the parameters of aesthetic representation. The era of proletarian power ought also to be a style period in the history of the arts. Following a line Gorky exposited at length in his speech to the Congress, delegates agreed the period would be characterized by 'socialist realism'.

The concept of socialist realism thus entered Marxist discourse in the context of a heroic mission in the face of existential threat, and at a moment of rupture in world history. Today, however, the phrase carries little but negative connotations. Socialist realism is associated with the substitution of political for aesthetic values, and the subordination of the creative individual to the authority of the state. In his *Marxist Aesthetics* of 1970 Leftist historian Henri Arvon sums up this view, writing that socialist realism:

> ... represents a bureaucratic and administrative conception of literature notable both for the exceptional vagueness and fuzziness of its notions in the realm of pure esthetics and for the implacable rigor of its judgements, which for the most part have no justification other than the political needs of the moment.[2]

For the musicologist, the term is all but useless as an objective style category precisely because its application so strongly connotes aesthetic failure.

Whatever its merits, this politically charged conception of socialist realism doubtless owes its prevalence to US propaganda efforts after 1945. Worried over the success and spread of anti-fascist, pro-Soviet cultural congresses (the international congress being the paradigmatic form of social democratic organising), the CIA funded the 1950 Congress for Cultural Freedom in Berlin. The

---

2   Arvon 1970, p. 83.

goal of the gathering was to oppose Soviet cultural policy on the basis that it represented a threat to individual liberty. As one historian hardly sympathetic to communism puts it:

> ... the Congress's endurance was [...] remarkable given that even its most dedicated participants agreed on little beyond their conviction that Communism as an idea and in practice, was incompatible with free intellectual inquiry.[3]

Largely through false-front organisations, the CIA continued to organize and fund anti-communist propaganda campaigns for decades. In the terms of these campaigns, the political question of party control comes to supplant the aesthetic question of realism in the arts, or even the historical question of the relationship between style and mode of production. Freeing the concept of a socialist realism in aesthetics from the role it played in the ideological battles of the Cold War is made all the more difficult given that official Soviet policy maintained its support for both realism and tendentiousness in the arts throughout the same period. The position was succinctly articulated by Andrei Zhdanov at the 1934 Congress:

> The truthfulness and historical concreteness of the artistic portrayal should be combined with the ideological remolding and education of the working people in the spirit of socialism. This method in literature and literary criticism is what we call the method of socialist realism.[4]

Furthermore, the category remained theoretically productive for art theory for an extended period as Mikhail Lifshitz's 1968 treatise on modernism, *The Crisis of Ugliness*, demonstrates.[5]

Given the centrality of the concept of socialist realism to both American and Soviet state propaganda campaigns, the idea serves as a lynchpin in the Cold War framework for understanding the extension of Marxism to the arts. Re-evaluating this concept, then, goes some way toward overcoming that framework and opening up discursive space within Marxism for an alternative approach.

Studies of Marxist aesthetics adopt a Cold War framework insofar as they sharply distinguish 'Eastern' from 'Western' branches of the tradition, as

---

3   Miller Harris 2016, p. 2.
4   Zhdanov 1950, p. 12.
5   Lifshitz 2018 [1968].

Merleau-Ponty does in his classic contribution to the literature.[6] The Eastern, beleaguered by the exigencies of state policy, is often presented as the corrupt twin of the Western. The latter, developed in relative freedom and informed by a Hegelian legacy suppressed by Stalinism, alone commands theoretical, rather than merely historical, interest.[7] What follows contributes to the undoing this framework by showing that the Hegelian strand in Marxist aesthetics is deeply informed by its Bolshevik predecessor and, crucially, shares with it a realist conception of art. Only after reconstructing the emergence and development of this conception – paying special attention to how music is directly addressed in the literature – can the compatibility of the realist conception of art with the materialist conception of history be properly assessed.

1 The Realist Conception of Art

The realist conception of art holds that artworks are a means by which at least some of their appreciators come to know truths about the world outside consciousness. Insofar as they are representational, painting, fiction, music and drama potentially constitute vehicles for coming to understand the world outside art. Artistic representation on this view is understood to be analogous to mental representation. Because genuinely representational, artworks can be called upon to complement the social sciences. Often, the realist conception is descriptive and normative at once. Given that artistic representation is amenable to realistic representation, artists ought to avoid generating illusions and, as much as possible, provide audiences with a reflection of the real world.

The prominence enjoyed by realist theories of art among Marxists in the twentieth century cannot be explained with reference to the work of Marx and Engels alone. Indeed, the founders of historical materialism did not leave their successors with a theory of art. Evidence suggests that taking up the topic was a relatively low priority for the revolutionary pair. When in their writing they departed from the critique of political economy and its philosophical underpinnings, Marx and Engels were most often concerned with polemicising about the natural sciences. Marx's mathematical theory, for example, is better developed than his thinking on art.[8] Their scattered writings on aesthetic topics, mostly restricted to literary criticism, cannot be said to point toward an aesthetic theory that could be expected to stand alongside, say, the value theory

---

6   Merleau-Ponty 1973.
7   This framing can be found in Laing 1978 and Arvon 1973.
8   Marx 1983 [1881].

of *Capital*. As for music, Marx very rarely mentions it. Engels did demonstrate some music literacy and an early love for the art (we have a botched chorale harmonisation in his hand, for example), but never theorized about it as such.[9]

Those paging through the *Collected Works* in search of the realist conception have often fallen upon Engels's reactions to agitational fiction written by his German socialist contemporaries. In a series of frequently cited letters, he critiqued their content for failing to properly characterize social phenomena relevant to revolutionary efforts. Ferdinand Lasalle, for instance, had in Engels's opinion failed in his 1859 novel, *City Girl*, to properly capture 'the revolutionary response of the members of the working class to the oppression that surrounds them, their convulsive attempts [...] to attain their rights as human beings'.[10] Here as elsewhere, Engels's interest in literary realism stems from its being a source for accurate sociological data at a time when few empirical studies – such as his own on the condition of the working class in England – yet existed. However, recognising that more or less useful and reliable knowledge can be garnered from the bourgeois novel is far from committing one's self to a fully-fledged realist conception of art.[11] Ultimately, the Founders offer scant resources for building such a theory.

Aesthetic realism moved to the centre of Marxist discourse in the twentieth century at the same time as realist approaches to the philosophy of natural science did. Both became the official doctrine of the most successful Marxist revolutionary organisation to come out of the period before the Second World War, namely, the Russian Social Democratic Labor Party's Bolshevik faction, the party of Lenin. It is something of a historical accident that questions of art and science should have so significantly concerned Russian revolutionists in this period. Indeed, the topic of realism emerged in the course of internal struggle within the party over its ideological directives.

The counterrevolutionary years that followed the 1906 revolution in Russia saw a number of influential Bolsheviks, Alexander Bogdanov among them, become convinced that the success of an anti-capitalist movement required that workers develop their own ideological institutions separate from those inherited from capitalist society. This involved creating both a proletarian art and a proletarian science.[12] To this end, Bogdanov, whose prominence in the

---

9   All of Marx and Engels's writings on music are helpfully summarised in Lindley 2010.

10   Engels 1972. How social history ought to be presented in literature was the least of the differences between Lasalle and the founders. Marx singles him out for criticism in his *Critique of the Gotha Program*.

11   For an alternative to my deflationary view of Engels's position on realism, see Lukács 1969.

12   Lynn Mally sums up the scope of the project's ambitions: 'Using the old bourgeois cul-

party at this time rivalled that of Lenin, established schools for instilling an autochthonous proletarian culture among party militants. He was helped in the endeavour by novelist and playwright Maxim Gorky, who offered his own property on the island of Capri as a campus. These schools became models for spreading the effort across Russia after the October victory in 1917. What came to be known as *Proletkult* was organized more or less spontaneously, which fit well with the movement's self-image.

As *Proletkult*'s goal was self-development, the focus of arts organisations was on the participation of proletarians in creative work. This was borne out in the musical realm, where educators organized to teach music literacy to workers, as well as to form amateur choirs and ensembles. Those trained in composition often entered the movement as composers of mass songs for untrained voices. Formal experimentation in composition came in the form of new genres, including the vocal symphony and the amateur opera. A paradigmatic example of the movement's musical face is Alexander Davidenko's *About Lenin* (1925). The piece consists solely of an unaccompanied bass recitation. Explicitly agitational, Davidenko characterized it as a 'musical placard'.[13] Far from being a dramatic representation of action, the stuff of opera, *About Lenin* is part and parcel of political work. It is meant to speak directly to 'proletarian aspirations and experience'.

For the movement's chief theorist, self-development in culture was not merely a means of empowerment or edification, but an aspect of forging a new proletarian reality. By the time *Proletkult* was in full force in cities across Russia (roughly 1920), Bogdanov had elaborated his own philosophical tendency, drawing inspiration from, among others, the work of the physicist Ernst Mach. Bogdanov took from Mach a thoroughgoing pragmatism with respect to ontology. Whatever can be acquired through the senses, from this perspective, encompasses the whole of reality. There is no need to speak of a world as it is *in itself*, that is, apart from human perception. All concepts are merely bundled sensory impressions. The shape these bundles take is determined by the tasks to which they are put in the course of human life. Bogdanov accepted Mach's conception of a reality organized pragmatically, through practice, and extended world-organising creative activity to encompass that of collectivities. Whole classes could mold the conceptual world to fit their historical tasks. In an

---

ture, create a new proletarian one opposed to the old and spread it to the masses. Develop a proletarian science, strengthen authentic comradely relations in the proletarian milieu, devise a proletarian philosophy, and turn art in the direction of proletarian aspirations and experience'. See Mally 1990, p. 8.

13   The musical activities of *Proletkult* are carefully analyzed in Edmunds 2000.

attempt to reconcile this view with historical materialism, Bogdanov held that relations of production structured 'living experience', and therefore the reality to which that experience pertained. His own rhapsodic prose is worth quoting at length:

> In labor and in cognition, humanity works out its own 'reality' – its own objective experience with its strict regularity and coherent organisation. The practice of this great social organism is nothing other than *world-building* [...]. This world, which has been constructed and continues to be under construction – the realm of the conquest of elemental spontaneity by life and thought, the kingdom of the socially organized elements of the universe – is the most grandiose and perfected that we know; it is the incarnation of life in nature.[14]

'Elemental spontaneity' in organisation, so key to the proletarian culture movement, quickly came under attack by the Leninist wing of the Bolshevik party. *Proletkult* existed outside party institutions and was not initially subject to their discipline. Independence was required for its cultural activities to count as proletarian self-development. However, this flew in the face of Lenin's concept of a vanguard party. Central to that concept was the party's duty to move workers to a class consciousness to which their own activities could not lead them.

Lenin understood the conditions of struggle within individual firms to be such that workers are compelled to bargain for as great a share of the value added by their labour as possible. This struggle, however, is structurally conditioned by the need for firms to remain profitable. The class consciousness of the trade union movement, the highest organisational achievement of the working class, then, was limited to workplace struggle. The goal of overcoming capitalist production as such, the core of socialist politics, had to be introduced to the working-class movement from outside its organically developed institutions, by a Marxist revolutionary party. In order to inspire labourers to secure for themselves more than just than a larger share of the value added by their own toil, the social democratic party would provide them with the conceptual and interpretive weapons with which to take political power and establish a socialist economy. The rational basis for building and maintaining a vanguard party necessarily implied safeguarding its monopoly on this ideological role.

Lenin's essay, *Party Organisation and Party Literature* (1905) offered a model for a cultural policy fit to vanguardism. There, Lenin insisted that:

---

14   Bogdanov 2015 [1913], p. 233.

... literature must become *part* of the common cause of the proletariat, 'a cog and a screw' of one single great Social-Democratic mechanism set in motion by the entire politically-conscious vanguard of the entire working class.

The arts were to become a 'component of organized, planned and integrated Social-Democratic Party work'.[15] On the 8th of October 1920, Lenin issued a statement that made clear his position on *Proletkult*:

Adhering unswervingly to this strand of principle, the All-Russia Pro-letkult Congress rejects in the most resolute manner, as theoretically unsound and practically harmful, all attempts to invent one's own partic-ular brand of culture, to remain isolated in self-contained organisations, to draw a line dividing the field of work of the People's Commissariat of Education and the Proletkult, or to set up a Proletkult 'autonomy' within establishments under the People's Commissariat of Education.

Lenin found *Proletkult's* organisational autonomy to be as dangerous a threat to Marxism as the philosophical anti-realism to which it was tied. He made his views on this latter clear as early as 1909 in his *Materialism and Empirio-Criticism.* That text polemicized against Mach's influence in the party, con-demning ontological realism's opponents for adopting an irredeemably bour-geois standpoint. Lenin's steely realism had consequences for aesthetics. While Bogdanov had thought that art-making ought to be part of the historic world-building of the proletariat, the Leninist view understood art's role as funda-mentally propagandistic. Aesthetic projects ought to inspire class conscious-ness among workers and peasants. As we have seen, it is on this basis that Lenin himself praised the German worker's chorus movement.[16]

By the early 1920s Lenin had taken ideological and political command of the party and sidelined Bogdanov. The proletarian culture project did not last through the 1930s. These conditions allowed a realist art theory – one that focused on artistic reception rather than production and that understood artistic realism to be tied to philosophical realism – to enjoy unchallenged prestige among Marxists from the 1920s onward. While Bogdanov had been concerned with the conditions of aesthetic creation, Lenin's focus was exclus-ively on the reception of art and culture. That focus would be maintained by

---

15   Lenin 1971 [1905], pp. 23–4.
16   Lenin 1971 [1913], pp. 225–6.

Bolsheviks well after the party leader's death in 1924. Embracing a reception theory of art allowed Marxists to see it as an extension of, or complement to, the sciences. Karl Kautsky articulated the view in his study of Christianity:

> Art [...] does not merely give us a photograph of reality; the artist must reproduce that which strikes him as the essential point, the characteristic fact of the reality he sets out to depict. The difference between art and science is in the fact that the artist represents the essential in a physical and tangible form, through which he impresses us, while the thinker represents the essential in the form of a conception, an abstraction.[17]

Art and science, then are two means to the same end. Both are purposively reductive in their representations, allowing for systematic reconstruction of the world as it is. So it was that throughout the 1920s the literary critic Alexander Voronsky could write of 'art as the cognition of life' while polemicising against the concept of proletarian culture. By the time the redoubtable Andrei Zhdanov came to impose party discipline on writers and composers in the Union after the Second World War, the realist conception of art was firmly in place.

The realist conception that acquired official sanction in the Soviet Union was sometimes defended without robust grounding in aesthetic theory. It was Georg Lukács, drawing on his training in literary criticism and academic philosophy, who provided this. His strategy was to adapt Hegelian aesthetics to Marxism. The Hegelian model allowed Lukács to maintain a Leninist focus on reception and realistic representation, while dispensing with a propaganda model for understanding the arts.

Hegel's aesthetics spring from his extension and transformation of Kant's theory of subjectivity. Kant had argued that objective knowledge of the world was possible only by virtue of certain non-empirical concepts that reside in the mind prior to cognition. These allow for experience to be gathered together into a unity, an I, that can become the subject of experience. The subject's knowings, its judgments (to use the Kantian term of art) are objective because they are grounded in the authority of a self-referencing subjectivity. The unity of consciousness and the knowability of the world are therefore inextricably linked for Kant.

Hegel departed from the Kantian model by demonstrating that individual subjects are not able to ground their authority as subjects in isolation. The

---

17   Kautsky 1925, p. 13.

authority of a unitary consciousness is a mere abstraction if conceived of as a function of concept use alone. Concretely grounding subjective authority for Hegel must involve winning recognition for that authority from another self-referencing subject. In a dialectical coincidence of opposites, true subjective independence is achieved through dependence. As Hegel puts it, authentic subjectivity is an 'I that is a We and the We that is an I'.[18] The achievement of recognition is won through struggle. In fact, Hegel first introduces his concept of recognition in his 1807 *Phenomenology of Spirit* as an analysis of the experience of mastery and slavery. Social institutions – from slavery to paternal authority, law to religion – emerge in history as a means of regulating the structure of mutual recognition and establishing a normative framework for the reproduction of a given form of life. Making use of a religious term he intends to desacralize, Hegel calls that normative framework 'spirit'. As subjects continue to struggle for increasingly concrete forms of freedom in intersubjective recognition, spirit can be said to mature through history.

Hegel distinguishes between two iterations of spirit, objective and absolute. Objective spirit refers to those institutions that are generally regulative of social life, but concerned with the practical, namely, the institutions of civil society, law and the state. By contrast, absolute spirit refers to the conceptual framework that binds and articulates a form of life as such. Paradigmatically, this includes religious, artistic, and philosophical institutions. For Hegel, societies progress historically by coming to self-consciousness about their spiritual foundation. Hegel's concept of 'science' is an attempt at precisely this: 'Spirit, *appearing* to consciousness in this element [as concept], or, what amounts to the same thing here, what is therein engendered by it, *is science*'.[19] The parallelism between science and art that Lukács inherited from Soviet Marxism finds its theoretical foundation here. Art in this system is like science insofar as it is a coming to self-consciousness of a form of life, a stage in the maturity of spirit.

Lukács was well aware that Marx's materialism was born precisely out of a critique of Hegel's theory of spirit. Marx set himself the task of replacing Hegel's speculative history with an account of the relations that human beings enter into in order to maximally manifest their always expanding set of skills and productive capacities. However, throughout his career Lukács was intent on making room for a Hegelian concern for consciousness within Marxism. In the essay 'The Changing Function of Historical Materialism', included in *History and Class Consciousness* (1923), Lukács insists that only a vulgar Marxism would

---

18   Hegel 2018 [1807], p. 108.
19   Hegel 2018 [1807], p. 460.

apply the historical materialist method to the study of those institutions Hegel groups under 'absolute spirit', art included. In a footnote, he defends his use of Hegelian language, writing that, while Marx did not take on Hegel's theory of spirit as such, he nonetheless had a notion of the unity of subject and object that could be made manifest in art.[20] Thus Lukács appropriates for Marxism an essentially idealist understanding of art as a form of social self-consciousness. What becomes self-conscious for Lukács is the spirit of a mode of production.

A maximally developed proletarian class consciousness represents the capitalist mode of production fully coming to know itself. That form of consciousness is the condition for the possibility of Marx's critique of political economy. It represents a shape of cognition that allows for a transition to a more concrete form of intersubjective freedom, namely, socialism. Because it is a manifestation of developed class consciousness, the art of advanced capitalism offers a reflection of reality without illusions. The proletariat's 'social being allows it [...] to transcend this [ideological] barrier and clearly see the class relationships, the development of the class struggle, that lies behind the fetishized forms of capitalist society'.[21] Thus, artistic realism represents the coming to self-knowledge of capitalism in the guise of absolute spirit.

Of all the arts, it is literature that appears most amenable to this account of realism. Indeed, Lukács's theory is focused almost exclusively on fiction. His theory, however, extends in principle to all the arts Hegel understands to be forms of absolute spirit, including music. Lukács himself, however, only rarely wrote about music directly.[22] Two instances, both from the latter part of his career, are instructive. The first appears in his two-volume *The Specificity of Aesthetics*. In the second volume, he acknowledges that music does not represent the world outside the self in the way painting and theatre do. It can, nonetheless, reflect the self's internal reality. In reflecting the emotional, affective aspect of individual experience, music is engaged in a 'double mimesis'. The inner world of the subject is a reflection of exterior reality, and music is a representative reconstruction of the internal logic of that reflection. Since he takes it that rhythm is at once part of the external world and an aspect of subjective experience, it allows music to link affect to worldly events. As one of his commentators summarizes the thought: 'In music, rhythm imitates the events, and tune and harmony are mimetic expressions of the feelings accompanying

---

20   Lukács 1972, p. 254.
21   Lukács 1981, p. 41.
22   A passage on music can be found in the second volume of Lukács 1963. Lukács also published an essay on Bartók, see Lukács 1971.

the events'. In this model, Lukács is able to maintain music's reflection of the exterior world while limiting its ability to represent social reality.

Another model is to be found in a 1970 essay Lukács wrote about Bartók on the occasion of the twenty-fifth anniversary of the composer's death. There, Lukács praises the Hungarian composer for having broken with an inherited concert music tradition, characterized by Richard Strauss and Johannes Brahms. That tradition is understood to be an ideological form of what Lenin called 'the Prussian way', that is, the reactionary coalition between urban capitalists and feudal landowners that followed the failed revolutions of 1848. By recognising the imperatives of addressing himself to the national question, inextricably tied to the struggle of the peasantry, and in breaking with his foreign inheritances and establishing an independent musical idiom, Bartók had successfully articulated a realistic assessment of the path of history for his people.[23] Presumably without having read either Lenin or Stalin on the national question, Bartók had nonetheless demonstrated musically what the revolutionary pair had discovered in politics. This account of musical realism is markedly different from the one to be found in Lukács's earlier *Aesthetics*. It dispenses almost entirely with the specificity of the musical while maintaining music's ability to directly represent the social and historical.

Lukács's uneven attempts to integrate music into his theoretical account of artistic realism were supplemented by theorists for whom his Marxist aesthetics served as a model. One such theorist was Lukács's fellow Hungarian and one-time pupil, János Maróthy, who developed the Eastern Bloc's most sophisticated theory of musical realism. In his magisterial *Music and the Bourgeois, Music and the Proletarian* (1974), Maróthy attempts to construct a theory of bourgeois music in a manner that is reminiscent of Marx's method in *Capital*. In the latter, the vast, diverse field of political economic phenomena is not derived from first principles, nor is it subject to descriptive generalisation. Rather, Marx's method in *Capital* is to reconstruct the laws of motion that regulate a capitalist economy from its own most basic category: the commodity. The commodity, split between *having* a form as a useful object and *being* a form of exchange value, is an empirical concept out of which Marx builds his theory of money, of capital, and ultimately of prices of production and economic crises. From the bare practice of exchanging equivalents, the nature of the capitalist system is unfolded. Maróthy adopts a parallel approach by building a theory

---

23   This essay ends: 'Hungarian culture must have the courage and social and moral basis to
       say: Bartók has opened for us the historical way to true Hungarian culture'. See Lukács 1971,
       p. 55.

of bourgeois music from what he takes to be its cellular form, the 'song'. This latter is a term of art in Maróthy. It does not refer to a musical genre, but to an abstract musico-grammatical structure that, in the last instance, regulates the complex reality of bourgeois music. While the structure of *Capital* serves as a reference for the Hungarian musicologist, the materialism in Marx's text is largely set aside in favour of a Hegelian framework.

Maróthy begins his long text by quoting the Marx of the *Grundrisse*, arguing that the kind of individuality specific to market societies arises on the basis of commodity production (production for exchange) rather than the other way around. The individuation of exchangers is a consequence of economic relations. Maróthy understands 'ego-centeredness' to be the fundamental ideological profile of bourgeois, commodity producing society. This ego-centrality is, for Maróthy, the shape of spirit proper to capitalism. As such, it comes to characterize the structure of artistic representation produced by and for that mode of production. What he calls 'song form' is the manifestation in music of that structure of the self which is specific to bourgeois productive relations.

By contrast, in pre-capitalist societies a concrete notion of individualism had yet to arise, and therefore no song form could develop. Rather, the music of pre-capitalist social formations was characterized by iterative and variative structures. These archaic forms were adapted to communal participation and improvisation. 'Song form', on the other hand, is a closed and self-referential structure. Whether performed by multiple musicians, or made up of independent voices, the form holds itself together as a unity, what Maróthy, after Hegel, calls 'a this'. Standing on its own, the song reproduces and represents the very bourgeois individualism that is its source and ground. It is a manifestation of absolute spirit under capitalism.

Maróthy's concept of musical realism is specific to this self-referential formal design. Song form is characterized by the presentation of musical material that remains recognizably itself through some transformation procedure or other. Ultimately, that material returns in something like its original shape. Maróthy's song is a game of identity in difference. 'The same as something else and something else as the same', he writes, 'is a problem at the centre of contemporary interest, which can appear either in the concrete shape of a picaresque novel or as a variation suite'.[24] Maróthy's musical realism involves the formal reconstruction in musical terms of the nature of individual subjectivity in an exchange society. In this way, it manifests a coming to self-consciousness of that

---

24   Maróthy 1974, p. 104.

society. As bourgeois music develops the potentialities inherent in its style, it comes to realize in artistic form the true nature of capitalist social relations. The analysis of that style and its history, then, becomes an analysis of bourgeois life, through its heroic early period through to its decadent fall into avant-garde obscurantism. Throughout, however, the interest of music lies in its ability to faithfully reflect social conditions at the level of formal design.

Transposing the locus of reflection from content to form is equally the achievement of Adorno's realist aesthetics. Despite his explicit rejection of what he took to be the hallmarks of socialist realism, as well as the principle of commitment in art, Theodor Adorno nonetheless embraced the core theoretical premise of the tradition, namely, that artworks are a means to the cognitive attainment of truths about reality. Although he arrives at his version of this thought by way of a distinctive theoretical apparatus, Adorno consistently maintained that artworks have what he calls a 'truth content'.

Adorno does not believe that an artwork enjoys truthful content by virtue of representing real conditions in a manner that is somehow artistically viable. Rather, the artwork in bourgeois society is not directly social. Instead, it is itself drawn into the social relation of the commodity form, in which the use value of products is of no structural importance to producers and the sociality of labour appears in alien form. Adorno does not, however, argue that artworks share the same commodified fate as washing machines and wallets in capitalist society. Instead, they are economically exceptional. He argues that 'works of art are absolute commodities; they are social products which have discarded the illusion of being-for-society, an illusion tenaciously retained by all other commodities'.[25] The way in which artworks have been shorn of use value draws them closer to the commodity form, even while they necessarily fail to acquire an exchange value determined by socially necessary labour time. The artwork's alienation from direct social use, its monad-like quality of windowless sovereignty and isolation, makes its relationship to society problematic.[26] Artworks cannot address themselves directly to social reality without giving up their sovereignty. At the same time, if they insist on their isolation, they do nothing but double down on the necessary illusion that sustains their status as commodities.

In order to arrive at truth artworks must express themselves 'as the wounds of society'.[27] Their alienation from human need is the ground of their ability to achieve truth in representation. When alienation becomes a premise

---

25   Adorno 1998 [1970], p. 321.
26   On the relevant notion of sovereignty, see Menke 1998.
27   Adorno 1998 [1970], p. 323.

motivating artistic design, the artwork is able to shed light on the 'the untruth of the social situation'.[28] Articulating a Hegelian coincidence of opposites, Adorno locates politically relevant, truthful representation in the unpolitical and abstractly formal. 'The liberation of form', he writes:

> ... which genuinely new art desires, holds enciphered within it above all the liberation of society, for form – the social nexus of everything particular – represents the social relation in the artwork; this is why liberated form is anathema to the status quo.[29]

Adorno's realism opposes itself to politically committed art of all kinds. In the art of commitment, which he associates primarily with Eastern Bloc régimes and orthodox Marxism, the enlightenment that comes through representation is negated by the formal conditions of that representation. These latter are in conformity with bourgeois society and ultimately reproduce the conditions for mass deception. Those conditions are spelled out by analogising art-making to the formation of Kantian judgments of the understanding. Kant theorized that empirical concepts require what he called 'schema', frameworks with which to graft themselves onto sense data. Formal design in art is, for Adorno, analogous to a Kantian schema. If cognising an object is entirely successful, because what arrives through the senses is perfectly amenable to some empirical concept or other, the authority of subjectivity – the ground of judgments for both Kant and Adorno – is imperceptible. By twisting its formal schema so as to militate against the material it forms, truthful art at once liberates material content and indexes the role of subjective freedom in an otherwise reified and alienated world.

Importantly, what is at stake for Adorno's realism is the same as in the other versions of the realist conception we have seen. In line with the tradition, he takes artworks to offer a kind of access to reality that is specific to their status as artworks, a realistic representation that complements the conclusions of the social sciences.

---

28   Adorno 1998 [1970], p. 323.
29   Adorno 1998 [1970], p. 255.

2   The Materialist Conception of Music History

The purpose of dwelling on the persistence of the realist conception of art within Marxism is to help clear a path forward for a revival of historical materialism in music studies. In order to make perspicuous what this entails, the key features of the materialist conception of history must first be made explicit.

Marx and Engels held that work and productivity are the ultimate drivers of change in the history of human society. A creative, ever-changing metabolic relation to nature is, in fact, necessary for human survival. Labor is presupposed by our biological makeup. For example, the human jaw is so formed as to require human beings to cook their food. Part of our digestive metabolism, then, occurs apart from our unconscious, somatic digestive capacities and exists fully in the realm of planned activity. Human beings, having no natural habitat of their own, are constantly in a process of reproducing and expanding their capacities for transforming their natural environment so as to suit their needs. Further, it is not in the nature of human labour to cease once the bare necessities for survival are met. The development of what Marx calls 'forces of production' (perhaps better translated as 'productive powers') entails the emergence of ever more sophisticated needs, including those that art-making fulfils. Forces of production encompass both physical and intellectual skills and achievements, and for Marx, they are at once the essence of humanity and the driver of its historical trajectory.

Productive forces are not exercised in isolation, but necessarily in human relationships of mutual dependency and co-operation, one of the most ancient forms of which is the sexual division of labour in procreation. Marx referred to those relations of mutual dependency as 'relations of production', and they manifest themselves as distributions of effective control over the means of productive labour. Importantly, relations of production – the power structures of social life – are adapted to the capacities they realize. For Marx and Engels, the direction of fit is from relations to forces. Maximising human creative potential is any given productive relation's only reason for being. Ultimately, social relations survive to the extent they foster, rather than fetter, human labour potential.

Marx considered the expansion of our capacities to be an amplification of our natures. As human beings develop the means of their life, they express their own essence. This is key to understanding Marx's critique of the mode of production organized by capital. In the capitalist mode of production, labour is not exploited for its usefulness. Rather, labourers are employed in production so as to increase the exchange value of the commodities that make up the means of production. The productivity of labour is measured in value terms. In capitalism, labouring produces more value than labourers receive in wages, and this surplus-value is the source of profit. Workers accept this exploitation because, having no property of their own, it is only by selling their capacity to work, their 'labour power', that they secure for themselves what they need to survive. As Marx spelled out as early as 1844, this estrangement of workers from their labour capacity estranges them from themselves:

> The relation is the relation of the worker to his own activity as an alien activity not belonging to him; it is activity as suffering, strength as weakness, begetting as emasculating, the worker's *own* physical and mental energy, his personal life – for what is life but activity? – as an activity which is turned against him, independent of him and not belonging to him.[30]

By reifying human labour and submitting it to market demands, capitalist productive relations set the stage for an immense increase in productive capacity. At the same time, however, they stultify and deskill the labour of the individual, who is severed from their essential productive powers and coerced into the production of value rather than utility.

Marx and Engels theorized that relations of production could outlive their usefulness. Capitalism structurally involves competition, which drives the constant revolutionising of the means of production, and consequently the aggregate of skills and capacities held by society at large. This social drive increasingly reduces the labour time required for meeting the needs of the species. Capitalism, then, can be seen as setting the stage for a quantitative reduction in labour time to solicit a qualitative transformation in social relations. These new relations would allow for individuals to develop their productive capacities for their own sake, in free association with others rather than under relations of production transmitted from the past and outside of their conscious control.

Within this framework, musical skills and achievements are best understood as a domain of human productive forces. Tracking the needs that musical capacities meet is an integral part of music history, but the point of interest for the historical materialist is the way in which those needs transform and expand. Like the other productive forces in society, musical capacities develop throughout history, and as they do, are maximized in the context of ever-changing relations of effective control and ownership. The drive that animates the history of agriculture, transportation, and manufacturing also drives the

---

30   Marx 1988 [1844], p. 75.

history of music making. The materialist conception of history offers no reasons for adopting a special method for the study of music.

Applying a materialist method to music history involves treating the art as part of the social base, rather than as an aspect of society's superstructure. This is a heterodox position among academic Marxists. The base/superstructure dichotomy that Marx outlines in the 1859 Preface to his *Critique of Political Economy* has frequently come under attack since the 1960s. The relevant passage from that text reads as follows:

> In the social production which men carry on they enter into definite relations that are indispensable and independent of their will; these relations of production correspond to a definite stage of development of their material powers of production. The totality of these relations of production constitutes the economic structure of society – the real foundation on which legal and political superstructures arise and to which definite forms of social consciousness correspond.[31]

New Left theorists in particular were keen to characterize this model as unhelpfully reductive since it explicitly affirms that consciousness is not ultimately determinative of the progress of history. In those instances when the model is not simply dismissed, music making is assumed to be superstructural, more akin to the law and the state than to the directly productive sphere.

Embracing the dichotomy, however, clarifies the materialist method. The distinction Marx is drawing is between the practices that are directly productive of social life and those institutions that are built to codify, sustain, and regulate such practices. These are paradigmatically legal institutions, but can be extended to include more or less informal regulatory norms. If what is being studied by musicologists is the practice of music making, then it is clear that they are concerned with something that lies comfortably within the boundaries of the economic base. The making of instruments, compositional techniques, ensemble configuration, control over intellectual property, and the like are all 'basic' in Marx's sense. Only the institutions that sanction and regulate musical production can be considered superstructural. Making the base/superstructure distinction clear for the arts goes some way to allay concerns that a materialist approach reduces them to a function of external, mechanical, and irredeemably 'economic' forces. On this reading, music making just *is* one of

---

31   I have used the Bottomore translation of this passage, which I take to be more accurate than alternative translations, found in Marx 1964, p. 51.

those forces. Further, the intellectual culture and normative institutions which correspond to those forces are, in the last instance, determined by the level of development of music making itself.

Setting music making squarely in the productive, economic realm demands that its specific mode of production be analysed in every instance. Some music making is homespun, made by and for its makers. Other music is made as small-scale craft production in which the maker controls the means of their production. It cannot be assumed that, even in the context of advanced capitalist societies, music is a commodity, made exclusively for the market and a bearer of value. A historical materialist is indeed committed to the idea that forces determine relations, but this is compatible with the claim that music's productive forces develop in a manner specific to the art and that the relations of its production are not always the same as those that generally reign in society.

A granular analysis of the modes of production in which music making takes place is often avoided by Marxist writing on art. This is the case especially among writers who insist that capitalism is a 'totality'. The notion of totality invites the assumption that capitalist social relations are all-encompassing, and that whatever does not occur in a value-generating circuit (Marx's paradigmatic M–C–M') is nonetheless somehow pulled into its logic. There does appear to be some textual support for this assumption. In a memorable passage from the *Grundrisse*, Marx writes that 'in all forms of society there is one specific kind of production which predominates over the rest, whose relations thus align rank and influence to the others'. He turns to metaphor in characterising this mode as a 'general illumination which bathes all the other colours and modifies their particularity'.[32] However, Marx does not claim that in bourgeois society, everything is subsumed under capitalism.[33] Rather, he is defending the method he develops in the *Grundrisse* and perfects in *Capital*, one in which the structure of capital is studied as if it were a kind of organism. The categories that order its logic are parts of a greater, self-moving whole. It is in this way that capital ought to be understood as a 'totality'. Marx distinguishes this method from a chronological, historical approach, which would fail to account for capital's special systematicity.

That capital is a system, however, does not imply that it is an all-encompassing system. A great deal of production takes place outside of that

---

32   Marx 1973 [1857–58], pp. 106–7.
33   Marx's account for the actual process of subsumption can be found in a manuscript titled 'Results of the Immediate Process of Production', which appears as an appendix in Marx 1976 [1867], pp. 949–1084.

mode. Marx himself pointed out that John Milton, who undoubtedly lived in a bourgeois society, produced his writing in a manner analogous to the way silk worms produce silk: for its own sake and as an expression of innate capacity. Much musical work is external to the self-valorisation of value. The private music teacher who sells her services does not advance capital. The civic orchestra that is funded through municipal taxation does not produce surplus-value for the investor class. Music making at church does not have to be bought as a commodity in order to be used by those who otherwise must sell their labour in order to live. Western musical life has given rise to three prominent types of capitalist investors: the instrument manufacturers, the impresarios, and the publishers of both print and sound recordings. All three have transformed the nature of musical production. For instance, piano manufacturers in the nineteenth century, pressured by competition, revolutionized the means of production of the instrument to such an extent as to bring the price of pianos to a level where they could appear in a great many private homes throughout Europe and the Americas. Those three kinds of capital, however, hardly represented the full range of music making.

A granular analysis of music's productive processes can even be the basis for explaining the evolution of the theoretical legacy that has attended music making throughout its history. The concepts that are relevant to music are a function of the specific relations of production on which its making is founded. So it is that the realist conception of art, say, can move from being the ground of a Marxist aesthetics to being a phenomenon to be materially explained using Marx's method.

In the end, historical materialism leaves little room for taking artistic realism seriously. Marx addressed realism very early in his career. His second *Theses on Feuerbach* reads as follows:

> The question whether objective truth can be attributed to human thinking is not a question of theory but is a *practical* question. Man must prove the truth, i.e. the reality and power, the this-sidedness of his thinking in practice. The dispute over the reality or non-reality of thinking that is isolated from practice is a purely *scholastic* question.[34]

It is unclear how any version of art realism could meet this standard. The reflections of the real that representative art offers are inherently spectatorial. At their most engaged, they can only be said to change minds. Historical materi-

---

34   Marx 1992, 422.

alism, on the other hand, aims at realism in Marx's sense. Its analyses are not validated by correspondence to reality, or by their capacity to predict future events. Materialism is realistic insofar as it participates in the transformation of social relations so as to bring them in line with the level of development of society's ever more impressive capacities.

Given its discontinuity with the materialist conception of history, contemporary Marxists should have enough reason to throw overboard the realist conception of art and abandon the attempt to bear witness to sociological truths in music. Further impetus for the move can come from evaluating the possible political consequences of adopting an approach to the arts that implicitly assumes the perspective of consumer rather than producer, and that focuses on traditional aesthetic concerns about form and content rather than the forces and relations of musical production. It is worth pointing out that the question of political consequences is only meaningfully asked in the context of socialist states. With few exceptions, 'Western' Marxists had little-to-no influence on mainstream political debate or on policymaking. If anything, it can be argued that the Frankfurt School's theoretical commitments were well-adapted to ratify political quietism.[35]

The fate of Soviet cultural policy after 1934 is a case in point. The speeches and resolutions of the Congress of Soviet Writers frequently endorse a Hegelian conception of art. They are helped to this in some measure by that much-quoted dictum (wrongly) attributed to Stalin that reckons artists to be 'engineers of the human soul'. Just as frequently, however, delegates would speak about musical development as a form of socialist construction. This was, after all, the period of the first two Five-Year Plans, which transformed the Soviet Union into a leading industrial power. The period of socialist realism as Congress delegates conceived it would correspond to a fully industrialized Soviet economy that lay in the not-so-distant future. Even while, in the realist vein traced above, he takes it that the arts operate analogously to cognition, Gorky can nevertheless offer up endorsements to the central premises of historical materialism. Just because these come from his pen, they are often bracingly eloquent. Thus, he reminds us that:

> The history of technical and scientific discoveries abounds in cases where even the growth of technical culture has been resisted by the bourgeoisie. These cases are commonly known, as is also the motive for such resistance, viz., the cheapness of labor-power. It will be argued that technique,

---

35   Freyenhagen 2014.

nevertheless, has developed and reached considerable heights. This is indisputable. But this is due to the fact that technique itself augurs, as it were, and suggests to man the possibility and necessity of its future development.[36]

A similar concern with qualitative improvements in the means of production – whether or not it is clear that these are the means of art-making – can be found in both the opening speech of the Congress and throughout Bukharin's remarks.

The discourse on cultural policy shifted considerably after the Second World War. The distance travelled can be measured by comparing Andrei Zhdanov's speech in 1934 with his post-war writings. When he served as Central Committee delegate to the Congress, Zhdanov had been a secretary of the CC for less than a year. He was a capable writer and a fine amateur pianist, but his service to the Union was carried out on the ideological front. Born in 1896, Zhdanov came of age with the revolution. During the Civil War, he stood out for his success propagandising Red Army soldiers. Throughout his career, Zhdanov focused on cultural policy in line with the widely-accepted assumption that the arts were not best understood as a branch of production, but rather as the terrain of ideological struggle.

By the late 1940s, optimism about the future of socialist construction had been replaced by fears of foreign threats. In a speech to prominent musicians in 1947, Zhdanov expressed alarm about two threats that faced Soviet music, namely, cosmopolitanism and formalism. If in 1934 he had praised the diversity of language in Soviet literature, now he urged composers to source their material from Russian folk traditions lest they betray some lack in that love of country which, he insists, characterizes genuine internationalism. He memorably adds that Lenin himself 'fought to cleanse our native tongue of [...] foreign litter'.[37] The threat of formalism, on the other hand, represented the malign influence of the Western avant-garde. Here, too, aesthetic failure could be corrected at the level of content. Zhdanov suggested that composers focus on program music, as representational success was the core of artistic purpose.

Histories of music in the Soviet Union sometimes refer to the decade between the victory over the Nazis and the death of Stalin as the *Zhdanovshchina*. The period was rife with conflict between the Union's leading composers and the apparatus of the Party. The reigning policy is even satirized in a comic can-

---

36   Gorky 1977.
37   Zhdanov 1950, p. 93.

tata by Dmitri Shostakovich begun in 1948, *Antiformalist Rayok*. The work bitterly pokes fun at just the sort of speechifying on aesthetics for which Zhdanov was infamous. Given that we have little evidence to doubt Shostakovich's earnest faith in socialism, we might be guided by his irony in concluding that Zhdanov's commitment to a realist conception of the art led him into a political cul-de-sac from which Soviet cultural policy only slowly and incompletely escaped in subsequent decades.

CHAPTER 2

The Cultural Phase of Industry

We have seen that Marxist writing on the arts has been saturated by the concerns of philosophical aesthetics and is for that reason largely exclusive of political economic categories. There is, however, one important exception to this rule.

The category of the 'culture industry' stands out as having been introduced in the context of Marxist discourse on the arts – indeed, on music in particular – while being taken up well outside the boundaries of those discussions. It finds resonance in pop culture, for example, and has become disciplinary common sense in musicology. In fact, the phrase is so widely accepted that it is no longer necessarily taken to denote a theory. The culture industry appears to exist with all the self-evidence of the arms industry or the agricultural sector. Writing on the eve of the Great Recession, the translator and scholar Robert Hullot-Kentor noted that, in a sense, the culture industry no longer exists. He argues that while the so-called 'schema of mass culture' was alive and well, homogenising our consumption and degrading our collective imagination, the frisson that ought to attend the disclosure of this phenomenon had evaporated. He writes:

> In becoming aware of the vanishing of the horizon against which Adorno's concept of the *culture industry* construed its meaning, we now recognize the exact – and only – sense in which it can be said that the *culture industry* no longer exists. The rubric of postmodernism delineates, as a marker in time, however indistinctly drawn, the boundary across which the perception of the primitive in us did not travel. The loss of this perception was not of one moment among many, but has amounted to an absolute diminution of historical perception that so depotentiated the impulse of the modern that it contracted to a well-documented art-historical period.[1]

Not only is Hullot-Kentor's observation no longer intuitive, it is an anachronism. The indistinctly drawn boundaries of the postmodern now find themselves in the past. The contemporary world regularly witnesses events which are best understood as barbarism. If anything, the political horizons of the

---

1 Hullot-Kentor 2008, p. 149.

present assume a classical, 'modernist' form. In light of the demise of electable centrism, the capitalist world might soon once again face a choice between socialism and fascism. One has reason, then, to conclude that if there is some trouble with the concept of the culture industry's sustained prominence, it does not arise from modernity's having been brushed aside by the progress of history. Furthermore, the category is particularly promising in the context of describing a materialist analysis of music history. After all, it is a straightforwardly economic concept, and tied to an empirical analysis of the mode of art production. What is left to be seen is the extent to which the political economic presuppositions that make the category intelligible are continuous with Marx's value theory.

The culture industry made its first appearance in Theodor Adorno and Max Horkheimer's 1944 *Dialectic of Enlightenment*. The book was a product of exile. In 1933, the authors, along with their colleagues at the University of Frankfurt's Institute for Social Research, fled Germany. Adorno and Horkheimer eventually found themselves living in an upscale neighbourhood of Los Angeles, where they penned their influential treatise.

Both the original text and the revised 1947 edition are dedicated to the political economist Friedrich Pollock. Pollock had been a founding member of the Institute and was an expert in Marx's political economy, as well as the economic development of the Soviet Union. He was also the originator of an unorthodox theory of fully regulated capitalism, a theory to which the authors of *DoE* enthusiastically subscribed.[2] Pollock understood the crisis of the 1930s to have ended the freely competitive phase of capitalist development. What supplanted it was a new phase of state-regulated capitalism in which a steadily diminishing number of large firms and financial institutions managed capital accumulation by means of the state. He predicted that, ultimately, any meaningful separation between the state and monopoly firms would dissolve. This regime would be able to avert the breakdown of capitalism prognosticated by Marx. It was Pollock's contention that in monopoly capitalism (or 'state capitalism'), economic contradictions had been superseded by political concerns.[3] As Gunzelin Schmid Noerr summarizes the view:

> ... there is in state capitalism no structural conflict between political objectives and economic necessities. [...] The planned economy has

---

2   Marramao 1975.

3   The term 'state capitalism' has suffered a particularly fraught history. It was used by Pollock and appears in the secondary literature. However, since it appears in the work of so many other theorists, I have refrained from using the term so as to avoid confusion.

become inevitable; the only decisive political question is whether it will be democratic or totalitarian, that is, the question as to how access to the administrative control of the economy and thus to the new ruling class is regulated.[4]

If in the competitive phase of capitalism economic relations were mediated by the political sphere, in the monopolistic phase political relations are mediated by economic planning.

Pollock's influence on Adorno was direct. Both authors contributed to the first issue of the *Zeitschrift für Sozialforschung* in 1932, and their essays pursue a common line. Even the titles they chose were echoes of one another: Adorno's 'Zur gesellschaftlichen Lage der Musik' [On the Social Situation of Music] mirrors Pollock's 'Die gegenwärtige Lage des Kapitalismus und die Aussichten einer planwirtschaftlichen Neuordnung' [The Present Situation of Capitalism and the Prospects for a Planned Economic Reorganisation]. The opening paragraph of Adorno's essay contends that:

> ... the islands of pre-capitalist 'music making' – such as the 19th century could still tolerate – have been washed away: the techniques of radio and sound film, in the hands of powerful monopolies and in unlimited control over the total capitalistic propaganda machine, have taken possession of even the innermost cell of musical practices, i.e. of domestic music making.[5]

His insistence on the total control of cultural production by monopolies is perfectly in line with Pollock's monopoly capitalism position. It is not an exaggeration to say that the culture industry chapter of *DoE*, written a decade later, represents an effort at working out the consequences for cultural theory of Pollack's political economy. Indeed, more than half of the references to monopoly capital in the original edition of the text occur in the chapter on the culture industry. Of all the book's claims, the culture industry thesis is most dependent on political economic presuppositions. Notably, at the time it was drafted, neither author took these presuppositions to be controversial enough to merit separate argument.

Adorno's adherence to Pollock's position is made more striking by the inclusion in that first volume of the *Zeitschrift* of an essay by another Marxist polit-

4 Adorno and Horkheimer 2002 [1944], p. 233.
5 Adorno 1978, p. 128.

ical economist, Henryk Grossman. His positions on concentration, accumulation, and crises represented an alternative to Pollock's. Grossman's major work, published on the eve of the Great Depression, argued that the existing Marxist literature up to that point had failed to properly interpret Marx's method in *Capital* and had, for that reason, given insufficient weight to his theory of the breakdown of the capitalist system.[6] For Grossman, Marx did not merely argue that capitalism is prone to crises, but that these were symptoms of terminal systemic decline.

He based his reconstruction of Marx's breakdown thesis largely on the third volume of *Capital*. There Marx shows that the ultimate driver of periodic crises is the tendency of the rate of profit to fall in the economy as a whole as capitalist industry matures. Marx understood the source of profit to be surplus value. In every productive firm, workers add more value to commodities than they are paid in wages. The surplus value produced in the economy overall is divided up among competing capitals, a dynamic that results in a general rate of profit for all capital investment. Because there are limits to how far a firm can extend the working day or intensify the labour performed by its workers, capitalists seek to slough off workers through automation. While individual firms who innovate in this way can secure profit margins above those of their competitors, this benefit lasts only so long as their automating innovation remains proprietary. In the long run, automation leads to falling prices. After all, a product's value is directly proportional to the amount of socially necessary labour time required for its production, and a commodity's price is indirectly determined by its value. While it is in the best interest of every capitalist firm to throw off workers, the process of replacing workers with machines leads to a decline in the average rate of profit, since exploited workers are the ultimate source of surplus value. The accumulation of capital – that is, the systemic need to constantly increase the amount of invested capital – is itself the ultimate limit to capitalist accumulation.

The breakdown thesis is not compatible with Pollock's conception of monopoly capitalism. Pollock's model is built to explain capitalism's resilience, and explicitly denies that there is any intrinsic limit to capital accumulation. Grossman's model interprets capital concentration and the rise of very large firms as a consequence of declining profitability, and therefore a symptom of systemic instability. Pollock interprets concentration and monopolisation as mechanisms of stability and guarantors of continued prosperity. In choosing to follow Pollock's lead on economics rather than Grossman's, Adorno and

---

6   Grossman 1992.

Horkheimer selected a political economic basis for their theory of culture that is at once less orthodox and more conservative. This is a largely overlooked, counterintuitive aspect of their work. In order to make it perspicuous, Pollock's position must be placed in the context of the development of Marxist political economy.

The theory of monopoly capitalism is not found in Marx. Rather, it is the product of Second International Marxism in the years between Marx's death and the outbreak of the First World War. In this period, conditions for the reception of Marx's political economy were far from propitious. With the repeal of the Anti-Socialist Laws in 1881, the SPD quickly grew to be Europe's largest working-class party. The adoption of the Erfurt Program in 1891 enshrined scientific socialism as the official theoretical doctrine of the movement. While it might appear as if, with this, Marxism had achieved its highest organisational expression, the theoretician's critique of political economy was only imperfectly assimilated by the SPD's leadership, and very imperfectly by its working-class rank and file. To a significant extent, this was because Marx's theory was simply not available in anything approaching an accessible form. The aging Engels, whose failing health and eyesight slowed the process of editing Marx's political economic manuscripts for publication, finished work on the third volume of *Capital* years after the Erfurt Congress. While Engels is often criticized for excessive alterations to the text, he retained Marx's dry, repetitious prose and tedious numerical examples. Indeed, his editions of both volumes two and three make for decidedly dense reading. Complicating matters for the reader are Marx's methodological innovations. The structure of *Capital* differs from that of all other major works of political economy and continues to be the subject of impassioned debate among exegetes. Sympathetic, clarifying texts on Marx's method did not appear until the twentieth century.[7]

What did appear before the turn of the century, on the other hand, were important critiques of Marx's work by unsympathetic economists. 1896 saw the publication of Eugen von Böhm-Bawerk's *Karl Marx and the Close of His System*, which accused Marx of having made serious logical errors in volume three of *Capital*.[8] While this charge did not go unchallenged by Second International Marxists, it nonetheless had a lasting, negative impact on the reception of Marx's work, especially his theory of capitalist crises.[9] In the early years of the last century, economists who did not tie themselves to the labour move-

---

7   See Rosdolsky 1977 and Rubin 2008 [1923].

8   Böhm-Bawerk 1966.

9   The best-known Marxist response to Böhm-Bawerk's work was that by Rudolf Hilferding. For a detailed history of the debate over logical inconsistency in Marx, see Kliman 2007.

ment largely rejected the theory of value that had been foundational for the discipline since its founding in the eighteenth century, and were thereby able to move the discipline decisively away from the critique of exploitative social relations. The pioneers of marginalist theories of value determination were among the most strident of Marx's critics.

With the death of Engels in the summer of 1895, some Second International theorists began to explicitly break with Marxist orthodoxy. Most infamous among them was Eduard Bernstein, whose 1899 *The Preconditions of Socialism* (better known today as *Evolutionary Socialism*) attempted to demonstrate that capitalism at the turn of the twentieth century did not conform to the predictions Marx had made about the system's development. A new phase had begun, one in which the tendencies to breakdown that Marx saw giving rise to repeated, devastating crises, were no longer determinative. Rather, a robustly self-organized, consolidated capitalist class could reliably prevent the system it ruled from falling into crises. The parties of the working class would have to reject their revolutionary strategy for seizing political power, as future conditions could not be relied upon to include moments of economically induced social conflict. 'The capitalist means of defense against crises', he wrote, referring to the formation of cartels, 'bear within themselves the seeds of a new and more onerous *bondage* of the working class'.[10] Bernstein's is a notable early example of a 'monopoly capitalism' thesis, one that certainly served as a model for Pollock.

It was not immediately influential. Bernstein's break with Marx became known as 'revisionism', and was roundly condemned by the majority of the SPD's public figures. In her famed pamphlet, *Social Reform or Revolution*, Rosa Luxemburg bitterly attacked Bernstein's position.[11] The formation of cartels and industrial combines, she argued, did not mitigate the crisis tendencies of the system, but rather intensified them. However, despite the pushback, the thought that 'monopoly capitalism' represented the end of an antagonistic phase of capitalist development continued to haunt the labor movement. Rudolf Hilferding, the Austrian political economist whose masterpiece, *Finance Capital* (1910), set the standard for Marxist economic analysis before the First World War, integrated the phenomenon of cartels into Marx's value theory. He focused on the role of financial institutions in eroding competitive markets and establish-

---

10   Bernstein 1993 [1899], p. 96.
11   Luxemburg 2004 [1900].

ing cartelized industries in mature economies, ultimately concluding that
the early century had witnessed the establishment of a post-competitive
phase of 'finance capital'.

While Hilferding did more than any other political economist of the period to
underscore the way in which extreme concentration conditioned the dynamics of capital accumulation, he vigorously denied that they could sustainably
regulate economic life. He writes that:

> Planned production and anarchic production are not quantitative oppos-
> ites such that by tacking on more and more 'planning' conscious organ-
> isation will emerge out of anarchy. Such a transformation can only take
> place suddenly by subordinating the whole of production to conscious
> control. [...] In itself, a general cartel which carries on the whole of pro-
> duction, and thus eliminates crises, is economically conceivable but in
> social and political terms such an arrangement is impossible, because it
> would inevitably come to grief on the conflict of interests which it would
> intensify to an extreme point. But to expect the abolition of crises from
> individual cartels simply shows a lack of insight into the causes of crises
> and the structure of capitalist society.[12]

Hilferding concedes that the formation of a 'general cartel' is, strictly speaking,
conceivable, even while he denies that it is politically sustainable. The case
against political feasibility, however, would not prove robust. The spectre of
the general cartel appeared again, weeks before the start of the First World
War, this time in an article by Karl Kautsky. Kautsky argued that capitalism
had entered a phase he called 'ultra-imperialism'. This phase would ultimately
compel cooperation among capitalists. 'There is no economic necessity for con-
tinuing the arms race after the World War', he writes, 'even from the standpoint
of the capitalist class itself'. He concludes that 'every far-sighted capitalist today
must call on his fellows: capitalists of all countries, unite!'[13]

   By the outbreak of the First World War, both the centre and the right wings of
Central European social democracy had adopted the position that cartels and
monopolies could and would dissolve the anarchy of market society. The very
large firms that had begun to establish themselves by the turn of the century
would bring production under the planned management of a free association

---

12   Hilferding 1981 [1919], pp. 296–7.
13   Kautsky 1983, p. 86.

of owners and investors. Such an association amounts to a perverse travesty of the free association of producers Marx had envisioned taking over social production after the demise of capitalist ownership. When Pollock takes up this same theme after the war, he is effectively reviving and updating the economic positions of the centre-right of the pre-war labour movement.

Thus, the political economic framework in which Adorno and Horkheimer develop their theory of cultural production complicates the widespread view that their work represents a 'Western' alternative to Second or Third International Marxism. Indeed, outside the context of their received Second International understanding of capitalist crises, their culture industry thesis is unintelligible. Second International orthodoxy has it that crises are rooted in the anarchy of the market. Disproportional investment in the various branches of production, a constantly recurring phenomenon given that firms are pitted against one another in competition, leads periodically to overproduction. When goods go unsold due to lack of demand, prices fall. This causes bankruptcies, not only among overproducing firms, but among firms who supply them with raw materials and means of production. Bankrupt firms lay off their employees, which lowers demand, causing prices to fall even further. General ruin, then, is a result of planned, rational calculation at the level of the individual firm, and the absence of planned, rational calculation at the level of society as a whole. If capitalism could disabuse itself of its competitive nature, the threat of ruin would disappear.[14]

Under conditions of monopoly, this is precisely what occurs. Pollock's planned economies balance investment and control demand, allowing capital accumulation to continue in perpetuity. Adorno and Horkheimer decry the consequences of this successful overcoming of capitalism's contradictions. Their concept of economic plan is all-encompassing. In monopoly capitalism, for example, even randomness is conditioned by planning. As the authors write:

> Just because society's energies have developed so far on the side of rationality that anyone might become an engineer or a manager, the choice of who is to receive from society the investment and confidence to be trained for such functions becomes entirely irrational.

'Chance and planning', they continue, 'become identical since, given the sameness of people, the fortune or misfortune of the individual, right up to the

---

14   Incidentally, the most concise and accessible presentation of this theory of crisis remains N. Bukharin and E. Preobrazhensky 1969, pp. 102–4.

top, loses all economic importance'. This is the essence of a post-liberal society. Monopoly has eradicated crises at the expense of liberalism's beloved free individual.

Adorno and Horkheimer's conclusions about the fate of culture under conditions of monopoly capital are decidedly bleak. While monopoly might have overcome the contradictions of the law of capitalist accumulation, it had not dissolved those of the law of value. For the authors, monopoly is a form of capitalism, and not a form of socialism, because goods are still produced for the purpose of exchange. The relative importance of exchange value over use value in determining the organisation of social labour gives rise to the appearance that exchange value is a property of exchanged things, an illusion Marx famously calls 'commodity fetishism'. If liberal capitalism had been superseded by socialism, commodity fetishism would have dissolved into irrelevance as needs became the primary determinant of production. However, since liberal capitalism was instead replaced by state sponsored monopoly, the law of value still regulates production – goods are still produced as commodities – even while it is now production according to a plan. Commodity fetishism remains firmly in place. The goods produced in society remain alienated from their direct producers, who sell their labour power to the state monopoly rather than the entrepreneur. Pollock had noted that a fully developed monopoly capitalism would need to establish conditions of full employment while preventing the consumption of the working class from excessively limiting profitability. While disciplining the consumption of the working class could be accomplished by police terror, it could also be achieved through ideological indoctrination. Given that the means of communication (especially film, television, and radio) are in the hands of economic planners who have the power to determine the content of their communications, advanced monopoly capitalism selects for what Adorno and Horkheimer call 'mass deception'. Because cultural production is no longer in the hands of craft producers who own their product at the moment of sale, but rather is made and distributed by the state monopoly, any possibility for the presence of critical content in cultural commodities is removed. It is no longer in the interest of any of the producers of cultural goods to include in them anything that threatens the social order or militates against the planned distribution of consumables for profit. 'The cultural commodities of the industry are governed', Adorno writes, 'by the principle of their realisation as value, and not by their own specific content and harmonious formation'.[15]

---

15   Adorno 1975, p. 13.

What lends this analysis its bleak pessimism is its static quality. The con- tradictions that run through monopoly production do not drive this mode to undermine itself on its own terms. Rather, the system can only be critiqued on the basis of criteria proper to liberal capitalism. Monopoly capitalism, then, has no inherent negativity. Having overcome the structural necessity of crisis, monopoly could only be transformed into socialism by an external force. While Adorno and Horkheimer's political pessimism has often been noted – and cri- tiqued – it is not often seen to derive from the political economic model the authors adopt. More than in the experience of revolutionary failure in 1918– 19, or in the descent of the world's first proletarian dictatorship into a Stalinist Thermidor, Frankfurt School pessimism is rooted in the assumption that bal- anced investment and economic planning have removed the material driver of revolutionary politics. The theory of the culture industry was formulated to explain how this fact also renders spiritual drivers inert.

The theory of monopoly capitalism does not allow for dialectical treat- ment. The system can sustain numerous structural infelicities while containing no internal contradictions. As Moishe Postone and Barbara Brick point out, this denies the theory historicity.[16] This feature of Adorno and Horkheimer's model helps explain why *DoE* does not trace a dialectic internal to the mode of production its authors believe is currently in place. That, for example, was Marx's project in *Capital*. Rather, the book reconstructs the tragic dialectic that transformed liberal capitalism into its opposite, namely, state monopoly. The Enlightenment stands in for the liberal order, with its competitive markets and periodic booms and busts, while primitivism and myth stand in for planned production for the sake of the valorisation of value.

We have seen how the theory of monopoly capitalism is assumed by the theory of the culture industry. Despite the inseparability of the latter from the former, however, the two theories have not met with equivalent fates since the middle of the last century. In fact, the theory of monopoly capitalism has not fared well at all.

It is now a consensus, not only among Marxists, but among Left political thinkers in general, that the capitalist mode of production is no longer in a state regulated, monopolistic phrase. The last half century or so is often referred to as a 'neoliberal' period, after the economic doctrine strongly associated with

---

16   Postone and Brick 1982. Postone's reconstruction of Pollock's political economic doc-
      trine is invaluable. However, the critical analysis presented in this article is unfortunately
      marred by Postone's vague, unhistorical notion of 'traditional Marxism'. Like Pollock and
      Adorno, Postone is a revolutionary pessimist.

it. This post-post-liberal phase is not characterized by cartels and state intervention, but by precisely the opposite, namely, free market competition and
deregulation. Adorno died two years before the United States ended the Bretton
Woods era and took the dollar off the gold standard. In the decade that followed, high unemployment and high inflation presented economic planners
with a situation that defied their theoretical models. Direct state involvement
in the economy was decisively rolled back in North America and Europe by the
end of the twentieth century, ushering in a regime of economic governance
that was indeed very bleak and pessimism-inducing, but not for the reasons
either Pollock or his culture theoretical followers could have predicted.

For all the theoretical consequences that followed in the wake of the economic changes just described, they pale in comparison to the shift in political
and economic discourse that followed in the wake of the 2008–9 Financial
Crisis. Any hopes that a post-Cold War, U.S. led, global capitalist order could
perpetually mitigate the damages of the business cycle could no longer be
held out. It is generally acknowledged that the global economy is currently
experiencing a long-term slowdown. Heterodox economics, particularly neo-
Keynesianism and Modern Monetary Theory, now command the attention of
American lawmakers. It is clear that, far from forging political power through
economic institutions, states around the world were not even equipped with
an economic framework that could adequately predict or respond to the crash
and its aftermath. The result has been a general discrediting of ruling parties in
the advanced economies. Given our conditions in the present, it appears that
neither a theory of monopoly capitalism nor one of the culture industry could
apply.

At the same time, theories of monopoly capitalism – of Pollock's variety
or any other – have come under criticism within the ranks of Marxist political economists. Anwar Shaikh, for example, has persuasively argued that the
assumptions about market competition that all Marxist theories of monopoly
capitalism rely on were not shared by Marx himself.[17] In order for monopoly
to be seen as fundamentally undermining the competitive nature of capitalist industry, one must presume a model of so-called 'perfect' competition, in
which 'a very large number of very small firms that are identical in scale and
cost structure all [face] the same horizontal demand curve'.[18] This assumption is proper to neo-classical economics and is shared by Keynesian theories
of 'imperfect competition'. It is not, however, found in the political economic

---

17   Shaikh 2016, pp. 259–71.
18   Shaikh 2016, p. 19.

doctrines of Smith, Ricardo, or Marx. Like classical political economists before him, Marx conceived of competition as an antagonistic struggle, one in which firms in the same sector ruthlessly compete to destroy one another. Mergers, vertical integration, concentration and the like are all tools in the competitive struggle, not deviations from an idealized normal case. Neither the growth of very large firms, nor their influence on government, then, is a sign that monopolies have denatured markets. Rather, they are the product of normal market conditions. Furthermore, it is not the case historically that nineteenth-century competition was closer to the neoclassical model of perfect competition. Perfect competition has no historical instance. Without neoclassical theoretical assumptions about competition, a post-liberal, post-competitive phase of capitalism is meaningless.

If the theory of the culture industry has fared better than that of monopoly capitalism, it is not due to lack of criticism. Even cultural theorists who embrace the usefulness of the category take aim at its perceived limitations. The theory's rigid determinacy, for example, is often worried over. The following passage from Andreas Huyssen is a case in point:

> [The theory of the culture industry] is not Marxist enough in that it ignores praxis, bypassing the struggles for meaning, symbols, and images which constitute cultural and social life even while the mass-media try to contain them. I am not denying that the increasing commodification of culture and its effects in all cultural products are pervasive. What I would deny is the implied notion that function and use are totally determined by corporate intentions, and that exchange value has totally supplanted use value.[19]

Huyssen takes aim at what he takes to be Adorno's reductive abstraction. While he concedes that the process of the homogenisation of culture is real, he denies that observed concrete conditions uniformly confirm this tendency. The process is incomplete and its progress turbulent. Huyssen chooses to see these moments of turbulence as sites of struggle. Notably, however, Huyssen implicitly endorses Adorno's conception of the monopoly phase of capital. The concrete, 'Marxist' struggle over symbols and images takes place in an economic context the critic trusts Adorno to have gotten right. There is, consequently, no talk of a struggle over what part of society exerts effective control over the means of production, musical or otherwise.

---

19   Huyssen 1989, p. 15.

A recent study by Fumi Okiji, *Jazz as Critique: Adorno and Black Expression Revisited*, similarly accepts the reality of monopoly. She writes that:

> [music] is never pure divertissement, even when it appears so, but is either a corroborator of monopolistic capitalism or a voice of dissent that immanently rallies against the socioeconomic order and ever-advancing rationalisation of modern and contemporary living.[20]

To be sure, Okiji is highly critical of Adorno's culture industry thesis, particularly the place occupied by American Jazz in the Frankfurt School theorist's critique of mass culture. Jazz, too, Okiji is at pains to show us, can be critical of our totalitarian conditions. She points out that 'jazz work is also able to present a prototype for alternative forms of social organisation'.[21] The form to which they are alternatives, however, goes relatively undiscussed.

To a significant degree, the theory of the culture industry has persisted in music studies by virtue of its abstraction from the political economic model that made it relevant. Adorno and Horkheimer are often read as critics of capitalism in general, rather than as cultural diagnosticians of liberal capitalism's dark, totalitarian twin. This abstraction allows a scholar such as Marianna Ritchey to make ample reference to Adorno in her recent study, *Composing Capital: Classical Music in the Neoliberal Era*, without mentioning the difference between the phase of capitalism she is interested in and the one Adorno believed to be in place and, in principle, insuperable.[22]

Going forward, we do well to leave the theory of the culture industry behind. Along with its political economic presuppositions, the category is now primarily of historical interest. Merely abandoning the theory, however, is dissatisfying. The question as to what theory of culture might correspond to a more sophisticated Marxian political economic framework is left open. While developing such a theory is well beyond the scope of this chapter, we can profitably turn to one of the first articulations of Marxist cultural theory for orienting clues.

Soon after the victory of the Hungarian Soviet, Georg Lukács, then a member of the revolutionary government, addressed the fate of culture in bourgeois society in an essay, 'The Old Culture and the New Culture'. Lukács defines 'the concept of culture (in opposition to civilisation)' as comprising 'the ensemble

---

20   Okiji 2008, p. 33.
21   Okiji 2008, p. 32.
22   Ritchey 2019.

of valuable products and abilities which are dispensable in relation to the immediate maintenance of life'.[23] Those who contributed to culture, then, were those who did not perform the labour that met the basest of mankind's needs. Those who lived off the social surplus were liberated from concern for the immediate maintenance of life and were free to pursue creative endeavours befitting free, self-determining individuals. The existence of culture depended on the maintenance of a leisure class. The industrial era, 'in surpassing the privileges of feudal estates [...] also surpassed the cultural privileges of estate society'. 'Capitalism', he writes, 'drove the ruling class itself, the bourgeoisie, into the service of production'.[24] These conditions led to a terminal crisis of culture that, Lukács maintains, had come before the final economic breakdown of capitalist society. Because 'liberation from capitalism means liberation from the rule of the economy', the coming of a classless society where labour is directly social means that conditions for the full flowering of culture will finally be in place.[25]

Lukács's optimism is thrilling. The image of the proletariat, from the moment of its dictatorship, inheriting the cultural legacy of all previous civilisations and building a form of cultural practice that does not depend on the exploitation of labour is heartening and attractive. However, it is not clear how, under those conditions, one might be able to pick out culture from the rest of human achievement. The demise of the division of labour seems to entail the irrelevance of the distinction between that which is done for its own sake and that which is done to support the immediate demands of social reproduction. Under conditions of common ownership, and with the establishment of a sharing economy, it difficult to imagine what might be at stake in separating cultural achievement from the meeting of human needs.

In capitalist society, the valorisation of value is accomplished for its own sake. Profit making necessarily appears as self-justifying, like art. By way of letting go of the worry over culture under capital, we could say that bourgeois society did not mark the emergence of an industrial phase of culture, in which the lofty aims of the mind were subordinated to the base needs of the stomach. The needs of the stomach often go unmet in capitalist societies. Rather, we can say that capitalism marks a cultural phase of industry. The social revolution, which brings to an end the divide between mind and stomach, hand and heart, can also be expected to do away with the content of the concept of culture.

---

23   Lukács 1970, p. 21.
24   Lukács 1970, p. 21.
25   Lukács 1970, p. 22.

CHAPTER 3

Disenchantment and Musicological Method

In the search for a materialist conception of music history, it is intuitive to begin – as I have done here – with the legacy of Marxist theorising about the arts. Unfortunately, the results of that investigation do not include a ready set of concepts that make extending the materialist analysis of production to music a simple and straightforward matter. If one searches in vain for a musicology in Marxism, then it stands to reason that one might turn to the legacy of theorising on musicological method to find a place for historical materialism. Such is the project of this chapter, together with the pair that follow.

Musicology is methodologically anarchic. The academic study of music encompasses philology, biography, formal analysis, and the historical contextualisation of individual works, along with a host of methodological turns assimilated from other disciplines. This latter category has so greatly expanded in the last half century that one scholar has referred to 'musicological omnivory', and associated its intensification with the rise of 'the neoliberal university'.[1] He argues that as the management of universities has come to resemble that of private firms – often directly the result of divestment from higher education on the part of the state – they have abandoned older habits of highbrow exclusion to fully embrace multiculturalism, interdisciplinarity, and hybridity, the ideological watchwords of the global investor class. There is no doubt that musicologists are influenced by the pieties held dear by the institutions they rely on for their livelihood, and this in sometimes startlingly subtle ways. In recent years, music departments in the United States and Europe have moved to abandon standard elements of their curricula so as to allow for maximal diversity in the scope, aim, and method of music studies. When not directly instigated by university administrators, these moves have in general been met with institutional support and approval. That said, the capitalist university cannot be held solely responsible for methodological anarchy in the discipline.[2] For one thing, a contest of approaches has plagued the field since its inception. Guido Adler's

---

1   Blake 2017.

2   The term capitalist university is preferable to neoliberal university, as it is both broader and more precise. Many of the features that critics of the neoliberal university index and protest are better explained with reference to the dynamics of capitalist production, rather than understood in terms of an opposition between private and public sectors.

    For an insightful history of the capitalist university in the post-war period, see Heller 2016.

well-known map of the discipline is at once an acknowledgement of musico-logy's extraordinary methodological pluralism, and an attempt to bring it under some kind of rational control.[3]

In his 1977 *Foundations of Music History*, Carl Dahlhaus admits that 'music historians [...] incline toward eclecticism in their methodology'.[4] Perhaps sur-prisingly, given that his book ostensibly aims to clarify music history's concep-tual foundations, Dahlhaus comes to eclecticism's defense. Music history, he argues, is, strictly speaking, impossible. For this reason, pluralism is inevitable, and even desirable. The contours of Dahlhaus's argument are not entirely ori-ginal, as we will see. Nevertheless, his represents a classic articulation of what many still take to be the music historical enterprise's aporetic nature.

1 Either History or Aesthetic Experience

Dahlhaus contends that music history's object of study necessarily appears to the researcher in the form of a vast collection of musical works. This is true even for music that was made before the advent of the work concept.[5] Dahlhaus's example is Bach's *St. Matthew Passion*, which is studied as a work despite the straightforwardly practical application to which the music was put, and des-pite its not being published during its composer's lifetime. To be sure the work concept is an ideal type, to which the historian may bind himself, consciously or not. It is also a concept that itself forms part of music history. It therefore confronts the scholar as 'an historical fact that he has to accept'.[6] Dahlhaus took seriously both the ideal types that regulate the practice of historiography, and the sustained relevance of inherited concepts. That said, neither of these is primarily responsible for the object of music history appearing in the form of works. It is, rather, music's status as a fine art that lends it this character. The fine arts consist of objects of aesthetic experience. The operative conception of aesthetic experience in *Foundations* is Kantian, so something must be said about Kant's aesthetic theory if we are to illuminate Dahlhaus's methodological concerns.

Kant's aesthetic theory is not primarily concerned with the arts, but with the mind-dependent conditions of objective experience. His model of object-

---

3 Mugglestone 1981.
4 Dahlhaus 1983.
5 Dahlhaus's understanding of the emergence of the work concept is thoroughly elaborated in Goehr 1992.
6 Dahlhaus 1983, p. 28.

ive cognition is a two-step process. The mind first constructs a representation of an object in the world using intuitions gathered through the senses. These must conform to the spatiotemporal conditions of mental representation. Then the mind applies a conceptual schema to its representations, bringing them under concepts. Objective cognition consists in this process of conceptual subsumption. The elements of cognition, then, are judgments, actions performed by the subject of experience. Importantly, in order for the subject to have the relevant representations at its disposal, they must display native unity: they must all be ascribable to an individual subject. Kant expresses this thought by noting that the 'I think' must, in principle, accompany all of our mental representations of objects in experience. Kant calls the subject's awareness of perception 'apperception', and so refers to a 'transcendental unity of apperception'. The unity of the subject of experience is a necessary condition for judging, and therefore, for knowing. It follows that a subject's conceptually mediated judgments, too, must hang together as a whole. Kant introduces 'pure' concepts (quantity, quality, causality, modality) that are not found in experience, but nonetheless must be employed in judgment so as to prevent the subject's falling into disunifying self-contradiction. If the unity of the subject falls apart, the ground of objective experience is destroyed. Transcendental unity can also be thought to stem from the active character of judging. As actions, judgements are deeds for which subjects are responsible. They are also commitments to which subjects can be held to account. This structure of responsibility indicates that Kant's theory of cognition is also a theory of subjective autonomy, which is to say, of freedom. However potentially counterintuitive the claim, Kant deems subjective freedom a necessary condition for objective knowledge.

Kant's conception of aesthetic experience is an extension of his theory of cognition. He notes that paradigmatic judgments of taste, such as 'this object is beautiful', do not amount to knowledge. Rather, these judgements are, in his language, 'reflective'. They are merely occasioned by objects that display certain formal properties. They originate in the sensations generated by the faculties of understanding themselves. When an object in experience is so formed as to be especially amenable to cognition, a pleasure is afforded the subject by the free play between our constructive faculty of representation, on the one hand, and our capacity to subsume representations under concepts on the other. This pleasure inspires a reflective judgment about an object's beauty. Kant has beauty in nature primarily in mind when constructing his theory. In particular, he has in mind the sense natural beauty inspires of having been designed. Aesthetic judgements respond to perceived purposiveness in an object's form, in abstraction from any given purpose.

If aesthetic experience involves abstraction, this does not prevent subjects from seeking intersubjective corroboration on judgments of taste. After all, our reflective judgments are made on the basis of a common set of faculties for sensing and knowing, a common sense, even if judgements of taste are not part of objective cognition. Dieter Henrich, with characteristic clarity, lays out what is at stake:

> The claim of aesthetic judgments] is justified because it is founded upon the same activities from which knowledge originates, albeit in a distinctive, interactive employment. Hence Kant first provided tools for establishing the aesthetic attitude as self-contained and autonomous, thus as the foundation for a conception of art that envisages art as a primordial way of being related to and situated within our world, a way that can neither be replaced nor surpassed by other achievements of man's rational capacities.[7]

The shift in focus within the Kantian paradigm – from natural beauty to art beauty, inspired by Hegel and others – is what grounds Dahlhaus's 'strong concept of art', which is, as he tells us, 'an intrinsic, aesthetic one rooted in immediate musical experience'.[8]

The trouble for Dahlhaus begins when musical works are treated as means for the pursuit of ends outside themselves. The historian or sociologist, for whom musical works serve as examples, as illustrations, or as raw data, does just this. The music historian in search of, say, a given composer's influence in the work of successors, or the sociologist who sees in a symphony the expression of political values, each treat the works they take up as means for pursuing their own narrative ends. This way of taking up musical works is incompatible with the strong concept of art, because it involves the suspension of aesthetic experience. Furthermore, the sociologist and historian often harbor a perverse interest in a work's parts, isolating these in their analyses at the expense of rendering a work's organic unity, the occasion for aesthetic experience, entirely obscure.

One might anticipate Dahlhaus's objection to the historian's practice at this point. The craft of music history threatens to become unintelligible if musical works are abstracted from the aesthetic experiences they invite – perhaps even demand. If our interest in music stems from just these experiences, once abandoned, it is not clear what motivations animate the historian. To the extent that

---

7 Henrich 1992, p. 30.
8 Dahlhaus 1983, pp. 28–9.

musical works are rendered mere material for historical narrative, they cease to serve as inspiration for its construction. Dahlhaus could worry that the practice of music history falls into performative contradiction. The practice would be no more rational than that of a surgeon who performs a life-saving procedure on a dead patient.

This, however, is not the thrust of Dahlhaus's objection. His grounds are ethical. 'The music historian who deliberately turns a blind eye to the discoveries of art theory in our century in order not to jeopardize the narrative structure of history', he writes, 'will forever be plagued by a nagging conscience, his aesthetic misgivings repressed or dulled but never resolved'.[9] The discoveries of art theory Dahlhaus references are doubtless those of Theodor Adorno, who is quoted extensively in his text. Ultimately, it is Adorno's post-Kantian theory of the artwork Dahlhaus defends. He might have had in mind a passage in *Aesthetic Theory*, published less than a decade before *Foundations*, where Adorno argues that 'artworks are historical exclusively by way of individual works that have taken shape in themselves, not by their external association, not even through the influence that they purportedly exert over each other'.[10] Adorno positions himself critically with respect to Kant's theory of cognition. He follows the latter in insisting on the inherent connection between a subject's experience of the world and that subject's self-identity. However, unlike Kant, Adorno resists limiting legitimate experience to objective experience, or what he calls 'identity thinking'.

Instinctively concerned with the freedom of the subject, the philosophers of the Enlightenment worried over the coherence of modern concepts. These are fully independent of traditional authority, inherited language, and the passive acquisitions of the senses. Any dependence concepts have on material mediation for their meaningfulness represents a threat to the self-sufficiency of reason. So it is that Descartes in the Second Meditation sought to demonstrate with a melting ball of wax the independence of ideas from the constantly shifting world of material appearances. When a ball of wax is cool, it is solid and yellow and sweet-smelling. When it is heated, it transforms into a brown, acrid, hot liquid. All of its apparent properties shift while the object remains the same, demonstrating that it is the mind and not the senses that has a genuine hold on objects. Post-Enlightenment scientific reason, following upon this insight, insists on the independence of conceptual authority from its material substrate. The authors of *Dialectic of Enlightenment* employ

---

9   Dahlhaus 1983, p. 28.
10   Adorno 1998 [1970].

the Weberian term 'disenchantment' to name this restriction of the rational authority of concepts. 'Thinking, as understood by the Enlightenment', Adorno and Horkheimer write:

> ... is a process of establishing a unified, scientific order and of deriving factual knowledge from principles, whether these principles are interpreted as arbitrarily posited axioms, innate ideas, or the highest abstractions.[11]

All concepts are subject to disenchantment and are, therefore, damaged concepts. This includes ethical principles, which, once disenchanted, are unable to motivate action. As J.M. Bernstein makes the point, 'reasons for action, ideally, would emerge from cognitive awareness of states of affairs; and in order for that to be the case a state of affairs itself must be capable of lodging a claim'.[12] If the rational claims made by material states of affairs are unable to mediate our ethical concepts, the latter are worse than useless: '[disenchanted] moral philosophies are acts of violence performed in the awareness that morality is nondeducible'.[13] Thinking with Kant, but opposed to his priorities, Adorno is intent on preserving the non-conceptual moment in cognition, sure that this moment is constitutive of the fullest use of reason.

What is at stake in aesthetic experience shifts in light of the inherent violence of a disenchanted conceptual order. The experience of the beautiful and the sublime are, in a sense, pre-conceptual. They are attuned to the claims made by objects on the faculties of knowledge, precisely what Adorno argues has evaporated from discursive thought. These experiences make no claim to be instances of objective cognition and so are not involved in the damaged use of reason. In *Negative Dialectics*, Adorno describes his philosophy as giving 'the Copernican Revolution an axial turn' away from the subject.[14] Kant had demonstrated that the ground of objective cognition lay, not in the world, but in the subject. Adorno's axial turn orients us toward the non-subjective in the philosophy of the subject. Because artworks induce aesthetic experience and resist complete subsumption under concepts – Adorno will insist that genuine artworks remain enigmatic no matter how well they are understood – they hold the door open for the full use of reason in an otherwise denuded discursive universe. The ethical stakes involved are clearest if we have in mind that the aesthetic claim artworks make is a species of material infer-

11   Adorno and Horkheimer 2002 [1944], p. 63.
12   Bernstein 2001, p. 203.
13   Adorno and Horkheimer 2002 [1944], p. 67.
14   Adorno 1973, p. 4.

ence, the kind of inference that would be required in the undamaged use of moral reason. Aesthetic experience symbolizes the possibility of an intelligible post-Enlightenment ethics. In this vein, Dahlhaus argues that 'objective aesthetic integrity finds its subjective correlate in moral integrity'.[15] Adorno locates the basis of that correlation in a parallel between the transcendental schematism that integrates diverse mental representations into the unified temporal order of experience, on the one hand, and the principle of formal coherence that unifies the elements of an artwork on the other. 'The processual character of artworks', Adorno writes, 'is nothing other than their temporal nucleus', as if artworks possessed the schematized unity of subjects. Understood in this way, artworks assume moral dignity. They are 'mortal human objects' that can 'pass away'.[16] They are also vulnerable to being demeaned if treated as a means to an end rather than as ends in themselves. Given that Kant's responsible and self-consistent judging subject has revealed itself to be a barbarian prone to violence, the mortal, human artwork takes on outsized importance. In an inhuman world, the artwork is morality's only hope.

2   Against Marxism

Living and working in West Berlin, Dahlhaus reckoned the most prominent and threatening brand of Enlightenment reason in his vicinity was Marxism. In his well-known essay on Dahlhaus, James Hepokoski writes that 'at the heart of the Dahlhaus Project was an effort to keep the Austro-Germanic canon from Beethoven to Schoenberg free from aggressively sociopolitical interpretations'.[17] There is no doubt that Marxism was the paradigm for this latter category. There are over seventy references to Marx and Marxism in *Foundations*, a book that only runs to one hundred and sixty-five pages. It would hardly be an exaggeration to call the book an anti-Marxist polemic were it not so very difficult to assess what Dahlhaus means by 'Marxism' when he makes use of the term. The early philosophical works of Marx and Engels are cited, as is a collected volume of their comments on art and literature. Apart from these, however, no Marxist texts are cited and no Marxists are mentioned by name. Hepokoski responds to the difficulty in interpretation by distinguishing 'orthodox or politically committed Marxism' from:

---

15   Dahlhaus 1983, p. 113.
16   Adorno 1998 [1970], p. 177.
17   Hepokoski 1991, p. 222.

... the far subtler traditions of Western Marxism (including such representatives as Georg Lukács and Walter Benjamin) and, more specifically, Critical Theory, represented by Adorno and continued (with a move further in the direction of Weber) in the 1970s and 80s by Habermas and others.

As we have seen, Dahlhaus could hardly have had this latter tradition in mind given his explicit and transparent intellectual debts to Adorno in particular. Hepokoski writes that the former category:

... includes Marxist-Leninist thought in the 'official', or Soviet/East German/Central-European sense; actively revolutionary or committed Marxisms (Leninism, Maoism, and various liberationist movements) as encountered among radical groups in West Germany in the 1960s and 70s.[18]

The distinction is of limited usefulness. First, however subtle and critical his thinking, Lukács was certainly a politically committed Leninist. Further, the Sino-Soviet split was nearly two decades old by the time *Foundations* appeared. Charity demands that we assume Dahlhaus could distinguish perfectly well between the theoretical positions of the Deutsche Kommunistische Partei (DKP), which succeeded the KPD after it was banned in West Germany in 1956, the Kommunistischer Bund Westdeutschland (KBW), the leading Maoist organisation at the time, and those found in Hans Magnus Enzenberger's cultural periodical *Kursbuch*. Having a capacious definition of 'politically committed' Marxism is especially problematic given that the purpose of Hepokoski's distinction is to isolate the specific theoretical tendency the Dahlhaus Project targets. Finally, the 'Western Marxist' tradition includes important music historical texts – examples include Ernst Bloch's *The Spirit of Utopia* and János Maróthy's *Music and the Bourgeois, Music and the Proletarian*, not to mention Adorno's musical writings – but neither Leninism, nor Maoism, nor the Third World liberation movements are well represented in the musicological literature.[19] It is therefore unclear how politically committed Marxism could be thought to offer a viable methodological alternative for the music historian. There is no evidence in the text to indicate that Dahlhaus meant to engage with Soviet musicology, and Hepokoski is justified in insisting that Dahlhaus's

18   Hepokoski 1991, pp. 225–7.
19   Bloch 2000 [1918]; Maróthy 1974.

concerns were focused on the intellectual climate in Germany. The reader is therefore at a loss to know how to interpret Dahlhaus's references to Marxism.

Anne Shreffler has suggested that the target of Dahlhaus's polemic is best represented by the work of Georg Knepler.[20] Knepler was the most prominent music historian working in the DDR at the time *Foundations* was written. There are clear parallels between the careers of both scholars, which might well have led Dahlhaus to see Knepler as his East German rival. The latter was openly committed to Marxism, both theoretically and politically, and aimed to engage with Western scholars, including Dahlhaus, on methodological issues. However, as Shreffler notes, Dahlhaus was loath to engage with East German scholarship in general, and so Knepler never appears by name. To be sure, a comparison of the two musicologists' methodological approaches is instructive, especially in the context of more recent developments in the field. For one, the scope of Knepler's work is expansive, extending from speculation about prehistoric music making (reminiscent of Gary Tomlinson's research on the evolution of the music making capacity) to popular and traditional musics, which have received increased attention in recent decades. In addition, Knepler's main theoretical publication, *Geschichte als Weg zum Musikverständnis*, resembles a great deal of current research insofar as it foregrounds sociology and the history of technology.[21]

However, reading Dahlhaus's anti-Marxist polemic as primarily directed at Knepler is problematic. Dahlhaus's references to the views of Marxists are not, for the most part, focused on themes peculiar to Knepler's research. Rather, they read more like stereotypes. 'Marxists', he writes, 'consider their histories objective precisely by virtue of their being partisan, since the cause they espouse happens to be enacting the dictates of Marx's "law of motion in history"'.[22] It is not clear what this last phrase refers to. It is not a quotation. Marx describes his critique of political economy as revealing the 'economic laws of motion of modern society', referring specifically to features of capitalist production, such as the law of capitalist accumulation and the law of the tendency of the rate of profit to decline.[23] Furthermore, the claim would be unfair if it were meant to describe Knepler's work. The only reference to Marxism in the latter's Mozart monograph, for example, is in the context of a critique of Soviet arts policy, hardly an example of partisanship. Incidentally, it appears oppos-

---

20   Shreffler 2003.
21   Knepler 1977.
22   Dahlhaus 1983, p. 88.
23   Marx 1976 [1867], pp. 90–1.

ite a page containing a favourable reference to Dahlhaus.[24] Some of Dahlhaus's comments are straightforwardly abusive. At one point he states that 'it is characteristic of Marxist history as a whole that it frequently reaches a stature in its theory – and in its critique of non-Marxist history – that far exceeds its actual attainments in historiography'.[25] This comment is decidedly uncharitable if interpreted as a description of Knepler's deep and wide-ranging output. At one moment, Dahlhaus distinguishes between 'orthodox' and 'vulgar' Marxists, without detailing who might fall into either camp.[26] Neither, however, is a fair description of Georg Knepler. However illuminating a foil he is for Dahlhaus, *Foundations*'s barbs are directed elsewhere.

In a footnote to his article, Hepokoski anticipates an objection to Dahlhaus's characterisation of Marxist scholarship. 'As current neo- (or post-) Marxists are likely to point out', he writes, 'Dahlhaus's anti-Marxist arguments throughout his writings presuppose, and then reject, a rather inflexibly formulated set of pro-Marxist positions'.[27] Shreffler admits that 'we can see now that the Cold War is over that Dahlhaus's position was ideologically determined too'.[28] These are misleading understatements. Given its dismissive tone, the lack of citations, and no obvious real-world target for his critique, we can conclude that Dahlhaus's anti-Marxism was, in truth, merely anti-Communism. As a historical fact, this is unremarkable. The Cold War context was hardly conducive to good faith debate on Marxism and historiography. More significant is the role the figure of the Marxist plays in Dahlhaus's defense of methodological eclecticism and the integrity of aesthetic experience. It is not immediately intuitive that the aesthetic experience of artworks requires any special pleading. Artworks are sought out precisely for the experiences they afford. Even in a world disenchanted by the pervasively rationalized use of concepts, aesthetic experience resiliently persists. The material, non-propositional claims made by artworks demand that we treat them as aesthetic objects, and on their own terms. Taking up artworks in a manner that makes aesthetic experience either irrelevant or impossible is, then, perverse. Dahlhaus's Marxist is committed to perversity as a result of embracing theoretical dogma and partisan loyalty. The figure is deployed to make palpable the threat history and sociology present to aesthetic experience. If the Marxist with his 'aggressively sociopolitical interpretations' is at the gates, Dahlhaus's defensive measures are well motivated.

---

24   Knepler 1994.
25   Dahlhaus 1983, p. 123.
26   Dahlhaus 1983, p. 116.
27   Hepokoski 1991, p. 240.
28   Shreffler 2003, p. 520.

3   Against Positivism

Despite Dahlhaus's deep and lasting influence on English-speaking musicology,
his explicit anti-Communism never became common sense in the discipline.
Meta-musicological discourse in the United States, however, did introduce a
figure who, overcome by ideology, threatens to bury aesthetic experience under
the weight of cold, formal rationality, namely, the positivist. The same year that
saw the first reprint of J.B. Robinson's translation of *Foundations* also saw the
publication of Joseph Kerman's *Contemplating Music: Challenges to Musicology*. This text is centrally concerned with identifying, critiquing, and offering
alternatives to positivism in the field. The rot set in at the start: 'Positivism
in scholarship was originally a nineteenth-century movement, a movement
which put its ineradicable stamp on early musicology'.[29] Kerman identifies positivism as primarily a philosophical movement, one that responded to the success of the natural sciences, especially their role in industry. If geometry had,
in a much earlier period, the status of model science, such that both the ration-
alist Spinoza and the humanist Giambattista Vico were compelled to present
their thought in the form of definitions and proofs, the natural sciences – physics, chemistry and biology – served to model knowledge production generally
in the late nineteenth century. The contributions of chemistry to agriculture
and of physics to engineering symbolized the identification of science with
industrial progress. Positivism manifested itself in the humanities as historians
sought to make their narratives as objective as possible by relying exclusively
on documentary sources. In music studies, the ideology took two characteristic
forms. One was an almost exclusive focus among musicologists on the production of critical editions of otherwise unavailable music. Once the dust from
these works had been carefully swept away by the trained musical philologist,
they could serve as the basis for generalisations and, eventually, the discovery
of music historical laws. In music theory, positivism took the form of analysis,
the application of abstract formal categories to individual works in order to
make perspicuous their underlying structure. Kerman cites Heinrich Schenker's concept of the *Urlinie* as paradigmatic for this kind of analysis. Schenker
followed Hanslick's lead in interpreting the positivist commitment to empiricism in music as a concern 'only with the internal relationship of musical
elements'. On Kerman's telling, positivism (or neopositivism, which does not
depart significantly from its nineteenth-century predecessor) flourished, especially in the United States after the Second World War, and continues to dom-

---

29   Kerman 1986.

inate music studies in his own moment. 'While musicology and analysis can be viewed as contradictory, even as rival approaches to music', he writes:

> ... both were well calculated to thrive in the intellectual atmosphere of neopositivism. The appeal of systematic analysis was that it provided for a positivistic approach to art, for a criticism that could draw on precisely defined, seemingly objective operations and shun subjective criteria.[30]

The persistence of positivism in music studies was encouraged by postwar scientism among composers. Kerman cites Milton Babbitt, whose '[language] is that of the logical positivists, from whose doctrine Babbitt has never been able to escape'.[31] The period of positivism's triumph was long, a full century, from the pioneering work of Philipp Spitta, to the style history of Guido Adler, through to the 1980s.

Kerman does not deny that positivist musicology made significant contributions to knowledge. Instead, he criticizes it for its decentring of aesthetic experience in the study of the art. He quotes Arthur Mendel noting that 'our interest in Mozart's Jupiter Symphony is different from the political historian's interest in Napoleon or the social historian's in the steam engine, [aesthetic experience] provides the primary impetus for many if not most musicologists. [...] It is an interest we can call *critical*'.[32] And, indeed, his own methodological prescription for the discipline involves turning away, firstly from inherited skills such as philology, codicology, and rastrology, and secondly, from formal analysis carried out for its own sake. Kerman argues on behalf of music criticism, a genre he takes to stem from our interest in music as an object of delight. The form of criticism he recommends is a musical analogue of literary criticism and closer in orientation to Donald Tovey than to Schenker. It is centrally focused on the meaning of a musical work, and employs history and analysis in the service of making explicit the fullness of a listener's potential interest in an artwork.

Kerman's meta-disciplinary intervention has a good deal in common with the argument of *Foundations*. Both Kerman and Dahlhaus believe that a crusading rationalism is fundamentally at odds with what Dahlhaus calls the 'strong concept of art'. They also agree that a science of music history is, for this reason, undesirable and impossible. Kerman's objection to formal analysis is even anticipated in Dahlhaus's *Analysis and Value Judgement*. Dahlhaus worries that 'theory based on analysis which it employs merely as means ori-

---

30 Kerman 1986, p. 73.
31 Kerman 1986, 75.
32 Kerman 1986, 32.

ginates through abstraction; the single case, the object of the analysis, appears as an interchangeable example of a rule'. As in Kerman, Schenker is Dahlhaus's example:

> The reduction to the same *Ursatz* of works with completely dissimilar foregrounds certainly pertains to theory – theory of rigorous character. The procedure abstracts. The analyses appear as means to support the hypothesis that significant musical works within the tradition from Bach to Brahms always are structured on an *Ursatz*.[33]

The illustrative analyses Dahlhaus appends to his text count as criticism in Kerman's sense.

While both authors employ the term 'positivism', they do so somewhat differently. Dahlhaus agrees that 'historiographical positivism' shatters artworks into their elements in its zeal to collect facts, and that the contradiction between 'contemplation and empirical enquiry' is fatal for the method. However, his examples of musicological positivism are primarily biography and reception history, not the production of editions. He also distinguishes between positivist scholarship and style history, while Kerman identifies the latter with the former.[34] That said, both thinkers understand positivism to have been a historical, philosophical movement with lasting impact on music research. Today, Kerman's characterisation of positivism and his narrative about its role in the field have long hardened into disciplinary common sense. It is perhaps for this reason that it is not often noticed that the scholars whose work is meant to exemplify positivism did not use the term to describe their methodological orientation. For example, Leopold von Ranke, a historian whose fame blossomed in the *Vormärz* period and who is often cited as a confirmed positivist – he sought to tell history 'as it really was', after all – did not understand himself to be participating in a philosophical movement called 'positivism'. His reputation as a positivist is largely the result of his reception by his successors around the turn of the twentieth century, and the identification was meant to separate his evidence-centred research methods from that of idealist historians.[35] The philosopher August Comte is credited with popularising the term, but a 'positivist' tendency in the humanities does not follow self-consciously in his footsteps. In fact, his philosophical legacy disappeared almost entirely

---

33   Dahlhaus 1972, p. 8.
34   Dahlhaus 1983, pp. 17–18. Incidentally, Dahlhaus is Kerman's source for categorizing Philipp Spitta as a 'crusading positivist'.
35   See Ross 1988.

from public consciousness in the twentieth century.[36] In this respect, positivism is unlike Darwinism or Marxism, intellectual traditions which are tied to a textual canon. The nineteenth-century scholars, such as Henrich Schenker and Guido Adler, whom Kerman places in the positivist camp, would hardly have considered their work positivistic. In a blow to Kerman's account, Kevin Karnes has gone so far as to argue that 'there never was a single, unambiguous positivist program upon which the discipline of musicology was founded'.[37] Leo Treitler has also questioned the usefulness of the category. In his review of *Contemplating Music*, he points out that twentieth-century musicologists who appear in Kerman's account as establishing and enforcing positivistic norms in the discipline would not have recognized themselves in that description. Oliver Strunk, for example, 'balked at attitudes that we can identify as positivist'.[38]

Kerman had been arguing for a critical method in musicology for at least two decades by the time *Contemplating Music* appeared. In 'A Profile for American Musicology', published in the *Journal of the American Musicological Society* in 1965, he writes that in a properly oriented version of the discipline, works of art are not studied as a means of furthering:

> ... the study of men in society. The terms are just turned around. Men in society are studied as a means of furthering the comprehension of works of art. This may be described as a critical orientation, to differentiate it from the sociological orientation.[39]

His vision for musicology is the same as it would be in 1985, but he contrasts criticism with sociology rather than positivism. Interestingly, this puts him even closer to Dahlhaus's position in *Foundations*. Given that Kerman's conception of positivism is so broad and not conceived in tandem with his notion of criticism, there is a question about its source.

The best candidate is the positivist dispute (*Positivismusstreit*) that erupted in German sociology in 1961 and continued, on and off, for the rest of that decade. It is easy to underestimate the impact of what appears at first glance to have been a regional academic affair. But, as Agnes Heller argues, the dispute was instrumental in opening up a 'theoretical public sphere', and not just in Germany.[40] This addition to the public sphere meant Critical Theory, and

---

36   Tellingly, the *Stanford Encyclopedia of Philosophy* has no entry for positivism.
37   Karnes 2008, p. 16.
38   Treitler 1989, p. 386.
39   Kerman 1965, p. 62.
40   Heller 1978.

eventually French structuralism and post-structuralism, could reach across disciplines and even find an audience among the general public. The terms of the debate were drawn by Adorno, who at a conference in Tübingen attacked the social sciences for failing to think critically about the data gathering methods they employ. He had questionnaire surveys and opinion polls particularly in mind. These methods appeared to yield maximally objective data because so little of their content was supplied by the researcher. Adorno argued that any pretensions to objectivity these methods have, they were blind to the social forces that structure the experience of the social world behind the backs of society's members. Given that the methods he sought to discredit were empirical, Adorno referred to them as positivistic. 'No matter how positivistic the modes of procedure', he wrote in his Tübingen address:

> ... they are implicitly based upon the notion – derived from the ground rules of democratic elections and all-too unhesitatingly generalized – that the embodiment of the contents of man's consciousness or unconsciousness which form the statistical universe possess an immediate key role for the societal process.[41]

Adorno maintained that the methods of the social sciences are insufficient insofar as they do not take seriously the special conditions of a commodity producing society. This form of social life has abstraction built into it. The specificity of the labour that produces use values is abstracted away in the process of exchange, which assumes that all commodities are the bearers of some quantum of abstract labour. This is not a matter of public opinion. Adorno writes that:

> ... even if a survey provided the statistically overwhelming evidence that workers no longer consider themselves to be workers and deny that there still exists such a thing as the proletariat, the non-existence of the proletariat would in no way have been proved.[42]

Thinking in the first instance of psychological theories of exchange and value, he stresses that the dialectical 'critique of this illusion has nothing to do with the positivistic scientific critique according to which one cannot regard the objective nature of exchange as valid'.[43] Adorno uses the term 'positivistic' to

---

41   Adorno, 1976, p. 84.
42   Adorno 1976, p. 84.
43   Adorno 1976, p. 80.

describe a philosophy of science that justifies shallow sociological empiricism. His aim was not to coin a term of abuse, but in his hands the descriptor could not help but become associated with the Frankfurt School's broader, Weberian critique of rationalisation. As the dispute about sociological method continued, 'positivism' came to mean a commitment to, and defense of, the damaged use of reason in a disenchanted industrial society. By the time Jürgen Habermas came to publish his *Knowledge and Human Interests* in 1968, 'positivism' could be used to refer to a whole series of philosophies of science from Comte to Karl Popper. In the wake of the dispute, any research methods that foregrounded empiricism and rejected dialectical reasoning could be described as positivist. Incidentally, Adorno and Habermas's counterparts in the dispute never claimed to be positivists and did not share Critical Theory's Weberian premises about rationality.

To be sure, Kerman does not cite the positivist dispute in *Contemplating Music*. He refers to positivism as if it were a fact of intellectual history and not an interpretation of history burdened with philosophical commitments. When Adorno appears in the text, he is cited as an authority on music, not as a philosopher. Unlike Dahlhaus, Kerman does not consciously aim to position his disciplinary critique somewhere downstream of Kant's critical philosophy. Rather, Kerman inherits his concept of positivism indirectly, precisely through the 'theoretical public sphere' the positivist dispute helped to open. As the productions of that public sphere arrived in musicology, they were interpreted as salubrious methodological alternatives to positivism.

4   Classical Musicology

Both the monographs discussed above are classics of the methodological turn that engulfed the field beginning in the 1980s, the so-called New Musicology. This 'critical' turn broke decisively from inherited research priorities. In a lecture delivered in 1968, Friedrich Blume argued that musicology ought to progress by continually shedding light on obscure repertoires. He insisted that the discipline 'is concerned not only with the "Great Masters" and with the most outstanding works of art but with vast masses of music still hidden under the debris of time'.[44] He worried aloud that questions of method could be overrated and come to distract from the discipline's pressing tasks. Blume the encyclopaedist would no doubt be dismayed by the proliferation of methodological manifestos in recent decades. Scholars have introduced musicologies

---

44   Brook, Downes, and van Solkema 1972, p. 27.

relational, decolonial, reparative, and queer, to name but a few. The New Musicology is not held together by a common set of methods, or by a common research program. Rather, what holds the critical turn together is its critique of rationality inherited, often indirectly, from the Frankfurt School. The need for methodological intervention is understood to derive from the failure and, ultimately, malign influence of scientific reason. If the discipline today is methodologically anarchic, it is so by design. Indeed, pluralism represents a hard-won achievement.

Nonetheless, there are worries that might stall an uncritical acceptance of the critical turn. In the first place, one might reasonably worry about the threat of arbitrariness. If the only criteria the scholar can draw upon to decide which methods to employ are (to borrow a term from Hepokoski) extra-musicological, then the selection would be determinate with respect to the scholar, but arbitrary with respect to the enterprise. In the second place, as we have seen already, there are serious inconsistencies between the musicological iteration of the Adornian critique of science and the facts of history. Dahlhaus's Marxist and Kerman's positivist are figures generated by the disenchantment narrative, and largely absent from the historical record. They serve as avatars for the force of Enlightenment reason. However much they clarify the stakes of the critical turn, they cannot help but obstruct a good faith understanding of either the discipline's origins or the potential methodological contributions of historical materialism. The former is especially serious, since taking a position on musicological method could only benefit from a robust understanding of its historical development. Abandoning the positivist label, we can refer to the musicological project at the moment of its institutionalisation as 'classical musicology'. Like 'classical physics', the term is neutral with respect to the validity of the model. It is also a historical concept, entailing conceptions of a past and a future. Musicological positivism can only be rejected and replaced, while classical musicology can be expanded, reformed, or developed. Adopting the phrase and its historicist implications can help clear the way for a sympathetic reconstruction of the logic of the science of music history.

The runaway success of the critique of scientific reason in the discipline has caused many contemporary musicologists to approach a figure like Guido Adler with a degree of suspicion that would be shocking if it did not go entirely unnoticed. One illustrative instance comes at the start of the opening essay of an edited volume entitled *Rethinking Difference in Music Scholarship*. The text begins with the following quotation from Adler:

> When the artist abandons the region of his forefathers in order to conquer a new territory, then the historian of art does not allow the old to become

deserted and desolate, but at the same time takes upon himself the dual task of assisting, with his army of helpers, the artist in the occupation by lending a hand in making the newly acquired soil arable, and setting up the equipment needed to construct a new work.

The authors read this passage as a transparent reference to European colonialism, and remark that 'few music scholars today would wish to think of themselves in Adler's terms, as auxiliaries in the service of empire'. There follows a reference to the work of Linda Tuhiwai Smith, a Maori scholar from New Zealand who offers a decolonial critique of the human sciences, insisting that they are 'inextricably linked to European imperialism and colonialism'. Adler's reference is meant to serve as further evidence in support of Smith's view. The authors go on to place their own work downstream of 'an extensive literature on difference and music that appeared in North American musicology and ethnomusicology' beginning in the 1990s. The implication is that this literature does not suffer from the imperialist ideological commitments that were presumably common sense to Adler.

This profoundly suspicious reading of the passage is hardly informed by history. To begin with, Austria held no colonies outside of Europe. Adler's essay did appear a year into Bismarck's colonial project, but was unlikely to have been much informed by it. Before 1884, the North German Confederation's chancellor explicitly rejected a colonial policy for the recently unified German state. What is more, European colonial policy between 1885 and the First World War was never uniformly popular anywhere in Central Europe. It cannot be assumed that Adler was sympathetic to expansionism or to Bismarck. In fact, given that what is known about his political sympathies – he was a feminist and a staunch internationalist – he is best thought of as a liberal. Further, 'imperialism' was not synonymous with colonialism in this period. The term emerged as a synonym for Bonapartism before it was adopted to describe the domestic and foreign policies of the British Empire. These did not just include the British occupation of Egypt, but also matters of economic policy. Bismarck's tariffs on foreign imports, for example, were paradigmatic examples of imperialism at the time Adler penned his essay. Finally, it is not clear that the passage in question could not describe the activities of a small holding farmer in the previous century. Adler's artist-farmer is clearly not a capitalist investor. The point of clarifying the context is not to argue that the essay's authors as bad historians – they are not. It is, rather, to exemplify the bias that attends contemporary discussion of pre-critical musicology. The authors' remarks on Adler are informed more by Habermas's notion of the colonisation of the lifeworld than by the facts of history.

Because the Critical Theory tradition frequently thematizes the role played by damaged, reified reason in making possible the rise of Nazism, some musicologists have understood classical musicology to have been complicit as well. Philip Bohlman, for example, writes that the latter has:

> ... a remarkable capacity to imagine music into an object that had nothing to do with political and moral crises, which we witness, for example, in the *wertfrei* confessions of European musicologists who had provided Nazi Germany with the necessary musical objects to eliminate those who would experience music in any other way.[45]

The grammar of this sentence makes for difficult reading, but it is clear enough that the author believes that an older generation of musicologists, having embraced a '*wertfrei*' method proper to the sciences, colluded thereby with the Third Reich. The word 'eliminate' evokes the memory of death camps. No specific musicologists working in Germany between 1933 and 1945 are mentioned, but none are likely to have consciously embraced the concept of *Wertfreiheit* with the religious passion implied by the confession metaphor. The term is Weber's, and is first defined in a 1917 text about method in the social sciences. Many, including Leo Strauss, influentially interpreted Weber as endorsing *Wertfreiheit* as a postulate in the sciences, although this does not turn out to be his view. The idea that scientific reason eliminates the intelligibility of human values is a major theme of the positivist controversy. Here, it is married to the critique of totalitarianism found in *Dialectic of Enlightenment* and elsewhere in the Critical Theory literature. The matter-of-fact way this author relates the science of music history to genocide is hair-raising. It would strike readers as patently unfair, even gruesome, were the acceptance of the Adornian account of scientific reason's malign influence any less pervasive.

A break with the critique of scientific rationality is a necessary prerequisite for making the adoption of historical materialism as musicological method intelligible. Such a break involves replacing the Weberian narrative so many music historians otherwise open to Marxism have assumed. Indeed, it is precisely the classical musicological project, with all its pretentions to objectivity and rationality, that is most amenable to taking on materialist foundations. The task at hand, then, is to reconstruct the emergence and initial development of that project so as to clarify the substantive contribution classical Marxism could have made to the discipline.

---

45   Bohlman 1993, p. 415.

CHAPTER 4

Democratic Formalism

In the New Musicology's historiography of the discipline, the figure of Eduard Hanslick plays an outsized role. In his seminal 1980 polemic, 'How We Got into Analysis and How to Get Out', Joseph Kerman cites Hanslick's aesthetic formalism as key to establishing the centrality of music analysis in the field. More than any other disciplinary method, Kerman understands analysis to exemplify positivism's ideological hold on the musicologist's consciousness. Bracketing music's historical context and intrinsic meanings, analysis is hopelessly formalistic, content to dissect a score as if it were an animal or plant specimen. What presents itself as an eminently rational set of procedures for making explicit the structural features of a piece is for Kerman an implicit endorsement of an ideology that is 'Viennese or Pan-German in origin, and certainly profoundly guided by nationalistic passions'. The undisclosed purpose of analysis is to cast in apparently neutral terms already established value judgments about the music analysed. Kerman writes that:

> ... for Hanslick, instrumental music was the only 'pure' form of the art, and words, librettos, titles, and programs which seem to link music to the feelings of ordinary, impure life were to be disregarded or deplored. Music, in Hanslick's famous phrase, is 'sounding form in motion'. [...] The concept is an important one for the essential criterion of value that is built into the ideology. For if music is only 'sounding form', the only meaningful study of music is formalistic.[1]

Two decades later, Susan McClary adopted the same narrative in her *Conventional Wisdom: The Content of Musical Form*. 'Theorists since the nineteenth-century critic Eduard Hanslick', she claims, 'have generally solved the split [between form and content] by redefining everything as structure – thus the institutional prestige of our graphs, charts, and quasi-mathematical explanations of music'.[2] Given the prominence accorded to Hanslick by those convinced of the critique of scientific reason, an alternative reconstruction of the musicological project ought to begin with him.

---

1   Kerman 1980, pp. 314–15.
2   McClary 2000, p. 6.

Eduard Hanslick's 1854 treatise, *On the Musically Beautiful*, inaugurated a new theoretical genre. Defining it, however, is no easy task. It is a not a work of philosophical aesthetics. In fact, Hanslick's subtitle identifies his treatise as a contribution to a revision of prevailing aesthetic views. His very first paragraph denies that beauty is the 'offspring of sensation [aisthesis]', a foundational premise of philosophical aesthetics since Baumgarten's 1750 *Aesthetica* set the parameters of modern discourse on the subject.[3] The book is also not a psychology of musical perception. Instead, Hanslick insists on determining the objective, rather than subjective, content of musical ideas. Clearly addressed to the musically literate, the text is nevertheless not a practical manual for the musician. Neither is Hanslick's treatise a historical study. In 1856 the University of Vienna accepted *On the Musically Beautiful* as Hanslick's *Habilitationsschrift*, which allowed him to become a lecturer despite his not being a philosopher, a scientist, or a professional musician. He went on to secure a permanent appointment in the History and Aesthetics of Music [*Tonkunst*] despite the fact that his most important book offers its readers neither a history nor an aesthetics of music. Impossible to pigeonhole, Hanslick's widely-read monograph is best interpreted as a bridge between two discourses. He offers the means for getting from German idealist aesthetics to a not-yet-developed science of music history. As such it serves a double function. It is at once a critique of the inherited conception of beauty and a propaedeutic for properly musicological inquiry.

Difficulties in classifying the text do not appear terribly serious if one assumes that Hanslick's primary motivation for writing *OMB* was professional advancement rather than scientific achievement. It is, after all, intuitive that an ambitious music critic, not yet thirty, should publish a monograph whose arguments conform to the demands of scholarly practice in the hopes of securing a teaching position. Naturally, those demands become less relevant to Hanslick after being named a lecturer, and indeed, he never further develops the theory he introduces in *OMB*. As Kevin Karnes has extensively detailed, he turned his attention elsewhere for the rest of his career.[4] However, to interpret the argument of *OMB* primarily in terms of professional opportunism is to misunderstand the nature of the professional opportunity Hanslick took advantage of. The two are not so easily disentangled. Not only was the lectureship he held the first of its kind, the position of *Privatdozent* as such did not exist at the University of Vienna a mere five years before *OMB* appeared in print.

---

3   Hanslick 2018 [1854], p. 1.
4   Karnes 2008, p. 4.

Both book and post are products of the revolutionary and counterrevolutionary events in and around 1848.

1   Failed Revolution and Liberalisation

By the middle of the nineteenth century, the Austrian state had begun to suffer some of the consequences of the failure of Napoleon's armies to eradicate
formally feudal government and administration in the empire. Austria in the
1840s was radically decentralized compared with France and Prussia. Despite
the adoption in 1812 of an Austrian General Civil Code, inhabitants knew no
uniform rule of law within the borders of the empire. Moreover, those borders
encompassed some of the most – as well as some of the least – economically developed regions in Europe. Steam engines employed in Bohemian coal
mines were among the first to be used in industry on the continent. By the early
1840s they also powered water vessels. Mining and textile manufacture in the
region made road and, eventually, rail construction necessary. Only about half
of Bohemia's population worked the land at mid-century. By contrast, modern
industry had yet to penetrate the eastern part of the empire. In Hungary, the
vast majority of the population farmed. Serfdom bound peasants to the land
and subjected them to constant expropriation. The persistence of economic
backwardness and feudal privilege allowed Austrian conservatives to hold back
the tide of political liberalisation that had reached other parts of the continent
decades before. Since it had not been made to accept constitutional limitations
to its authority, there existed no formal checks to the power of the crown, and it
acknowledged no civil rights. Limits to state power were matters of fact rather
than of law, and these proved to be significant in 1848 when the head of state
was forced to flee the capitol twice over before the end of that year.

Ecclesiastical power complemented absolutist rule. Religious indoctrination was indispensable to the smooth functioning of a state that could not
always rely on fear of worldly violence to establish its authority. With no separation of church and state, the former served as an organ of the latter, which
trained and appointed the clergy. Training for civil service was the primary
purpose of the empire's system of higher education. Universities were therefore teaching institutions, not centres of research, and curricula were closely
monitored by state officials. Alongside priests, these institutions credentialed
teachers, medical professionals, and lawyers. Professors who did not find themselves on the faculties of theology, medicine, or jurisprudence were relegated
to the faculty of philosophy. This latter was markedly subordinate to those of
the professional schools. The natural sciences – pursued in Bohemia more fer-

vently than in Vienna – were often auxiliary to the study of medicine. With very few exceptions, Austria produced little in the way of internationally recognized scholarship and research. Indeed, many scientists born in the empire chose to make their careers abroad. The decidedly backward situation of higher education displeased even those who admired and supported the autocracy it served. In 1819 Count Metternich had been instrumental in the issuing the Carlsbad Decrees which, along with cracking down on non-aristocratic student self-organisation and leading to the expulsion of liberal faculty members, placed representatives of the state in university classrooms to ensure that what was taught there was sanctioned by royal authority. Decades later, the same Count Metternich complained of Austria's 'reputation of obscurantism'.[5]

The conditions that upheld obscurantism were ultimately broken by the force of student revolts inspired by news of the overthrow of the July Monarchy in France. In Vienna, university students represented the most militant fraction of the revolution's social base. The demographic boom that picked up after the end of the Napoleonic Wars did not coincide with the growth of the Austrian state. The number of posts was not commensurate to the number of graduates, and by the 1840s their patience with a transparently sclerotic state education system had run out. Its legitimacy among the student body depended on the promise of upward social mobility through professionalisation. As the credibility of this promise wore thin, students turned to radical, democratic demands. Foremost among these were the freedom of teaching and learning [*Lern- und Lehrfreiheit*] and participation in the selection of university leadership. The call for new academic freedoms was joined to broader political demands that, among other things, would serve to secure and guarantee the former. In the context of a supranational imperial regime, this inevitably meant the overthrow of the state and the declaration of a republic. The economic frustration that faced students had much in common with that which confronted most skilled artisans. Fully trained craft producers increasingly found it impossible to rise to the status of Master in a society in which, unlike in post-Revolutionary France, guild organisation remained widespread and powerful. Further, artisans faced direct threats to their livelihood posed by both merchant and productive capital. Merchants exerted expanded control over small producers through the putting-out system at the same time as new industrial products came to dominate the market for the goods artisans traditionally supplied. Students and skilled workers shared a common horror of falling into the growing ranks of propertyless labourers. The industrial proletariat in Central

---

5   Höflechner 2017, p. 19.

Europe in this period was small, disorganized, desperately poor and routinely migratory. When German townsfolk and peasants in Baden, just east of the Rhine, received word of the revolution in Paris, paranoid hysteria overtook a population who feared not only another French invasion, but also the mass return of German workers who had migrated to Alsace in times of economic growth, but who now found themselves unemployed by the economic contraction of the 1840s. In the view of most, the unemployed proletarian presented as much a danger to society as an invading French soldier.

Workers and students faced off against mercenary troops in street battles in March. The empire's capacity for physical repression was limited and student demands to be issued arms for self-defence were eventually met. Benefit concerts were organized to help fund the student militants. For the next year, it was conceivable that the empire might fall. However, a reversal of fortunes for regrouped forces of reaction came swiftly by the end of 1848. Democratic forces had neither the ideological consistency, nor the organisational discipline, nor the requisite popular support to take power in the civil conflicts. For the monarchy, reconstituting the state in the wake of the failed revolutions could not avoid granting concessions. These were largely not political. The constitution adopted in the first months of 1849 was immediately suspended and later abandoned. The franchise was not radically expanded. There were important economic reforms: most notably, the abolition of serfdom throughout the empire. The reforms that concern us here, however, were those made to the structure of the Austrian university. These were spearheaded by one Count Leo von Thun, and have come to be known as the Thunian Reforms. Count Thun was no republican, but neither were his political commitments uniformly conservative. He advocated for modernisation, maintained strong sympathies for Czech nationalism, and supported broad reforms to the education system. The changes that began in 1849 brought the university under faculty control, eliminating direct state intervention in curricular design. The student demand for freedom of teaching and learning was met. Meeting it involved introducing the position of private lecturer, as well as university staff fees to fund it The result was to expand the range of scientific research and teaching. Among the goals of Thun's reforms was to increase the relative importance of the philosophical faculty vis-à-vis the professional faculty. Much of the teaching responsibilities of the former would become part of a more robust secondary school curriculum. As a whole, the Austrian university would begin a long transition from a teaching institution training members of what was, in effect, a state bureaucracy, to a modern research university on the Humboltian model.

Hanslick's time as a student in Vienna coincided with these events. He graduated from the university in 1849, just as many of the Thunian reforms began to take effect. As a student, Hanslick adopted the political sympathies of his social peers, which at the time entailed a bourgeois rejection of aristocracy, a principled embrace of democracy, and a commitment to national unity. As Hiroshi Yoshida has shown, far from being aloof from politics as he would sometimes claim he had been in later life, the young Hanslick was an enthusiastic supporter of the revolutionary movement. Describing a demonstration in front of the Stephansdom in March of 1848, Hanslick insisted that the singing of *Was ist des Deutschen Vaterland?*, a many-versed tune celebrating German national unity, was 'more than a concert, it was a deed'.[6] The description is notable given the mediocrity of the song itself. Hanslick's musical writings from the 1840s not only express bourgeois liberalism, but also endorse Hegelian aesthetic commitments. Hegel was dead by 1831 and his academic position in Berlin had gone to F.W.J. Schelling, a philosophical rival. His influence on the Left in the 1840s, however, was pervasive, and this can in large part be attributed to his conception of historicity. Hegel broke with his predecessors in tying rational justification for normative content of all kinds – logical, ethical, legal, aesthetic – to the process of its historical emergence and development. In fact, an analysis of the latter, if it is of the right kind, can serve as the former. Political progressives found in Hegel's historicism the means for grounding demands for the recognition of new social and legal norms. Hegel's account of the disclosive power of artworks maintains that in a philosophically relevant, but nonetheless non-discursive way, art allows the historical conditions of mindedness that allowed for its creation to be subjectively comprehended. In this way, art mirrors philosophy, which Hegel claims 'is its own time comprehended in thought'. Compared to Hegel's aesthetic historicism, the formalism of *OMB* can appear startlingly conservative. In fact, the claim that he reverted to a neo-Kantian line after 1849 is a commonplace in the secondary literature, leading scholars to offer explanations for his philosophical retreat. Even Hanslick's turn against Wagner has, however oddly, been interpreted as rightward drift.

Hanslick ultimately turned his back on his youthful enthusiasm for political song, but he never abandoned the liberal, progressive politics that motivated it. His mature view of the period can be read in his 1870 *Geschichte des Conzertswesens in Wien* [The History of Concert Life in Vienna]. There he argues that music making in the city had fallen into decadence in the pre-March period. Italian opera and virtuoso concertising dominated musical life, and not just in terms of taste. The state granted performance privileges to select theatre directors and suppressed competing performances. Musical concerts could be given at noon,

---

6   Yoshida 2001, p. 187.

and lower entertainments, like circus acts, would be allowed to proceed in the afternoon. Given that touring virtuosi could expect to make a healthy profit from ticket sales, they could afford to pay a fee in exchange for permission to perform. Other forms of music making were relegated to the private sphere, which severely limited their capacity. The aristocratic system of musical patronage and privilege came under direct attack with the onset of the revolution. Placards announcing the upcoming season of Italian opera were defaced and singers fled the city. The stages and concert halls of the city went dark as the streets burst into song. The Hanslick of 1870 can barely contain his contempt for the politically engaged music that enjoyed sudden mass appeal. At one point he remarks that the political spring had reversed the order of nature, sowing musical seeds that grew into fertilizer. Hanslick maintains that the revolution did not immediately give rise to a new musical culture, and could not have. In fact, for a time, the events made genuine concert life impossible. Nonetheless, he calls the failed revolution a 'world-historical experience', and likens it to Tamino's trials in *The Magic Flute*. Two decades after the fact, Hanslick saw that the uprisings had allowed for the modernising of the Austrian musical system. The same year *OMB* was published, the Viennese police stopped enforcing theatre directors' privileges. The quality of concerts increased and the seriousness of the repertoire deepened. Despite his objections to their work, Hanslick cites more frequent and better performances of Berlioz and Wagner as evidence that Viennese concert life has entered a new and progressive historical phase. At the centre of Hanslick's conception of the new moment is the expansion of musical knowledge, especially historical knowledge. He celebrates the appearance of scholarly Bach and Handel editions. He writes that the:

> ... tendency to revive the musical treasures of the past vividly recalls the ideal aspirations of that epoch of humanism and the revival of the art and science of antiquity, which in cultural history is simply called 'the Renaissance'.[7]

A music historical optimist, Hanslick is sanguine about the ability of political freedoms to stimulate musical development.

Hanslick mentions his own university appointment as further evidence of progress. Civil society organs for the development and performance of music

---

7 'Diese Tendenz nach Wiederbelebung der musikalischen Schätze der Vergangenheit erinnert lebhaft an die idealen Bestrebungen jener Epoche des Humanismus und der Wiedererweckung von Kunst und Wissenschaft des Alterthums, welche in der Culturgeschichte kurzweg "die Renaissance" heisst'. See Hanslick 1869, p. 427.

had been an increasingly common feature of German civic life since the end of the Continental Wars. Mendelssohn's wildly successful revival performance of Bach's *St. Matthew Passion* in 1829 stands out as a paradigm for bourgeois musical self-organisation. Just as scientists, doctors and students had been organising themselves into societies for the promotion of their careers since the early decades of the century, musicians had been freely associating to study and perform both new and ancient music. The freedom of teaching and learning after 1849 meant that some of these civil society driven development projects could be brought into the university system. The establishment of research institutes, another Thunian innovation, smoothed the transition. In 1851, the Central Institute for Meteorology and Earth Magnetism became the first state weather service in the world. When the Institute for Musicology was established in 1901, it exemplified a process of liberalisation that had been proceeding for half a century.

2   Discursivity and the Authority of Musical Norms

Despite Hanslick having granted him only a single mention in *OMB* – and that in passing – there is no doubt that Kant's critical philosophy hovers over the text like a ghost. His influence is widely acknowledged and can be read in the role of the imagination in the argument, the author's embrace of aesthetic formalism, as well as his characteristically Kantian use of the concept of 'pathology'. That said, if Hanslick was no longer a Somewhat Left Hegelian after 1848, he had not become a neo-Kantian. That intellectual movement postdates the publication of *OMB* by several decades. In recent years, scholars have pushed back against a long tradition of associating *OMB* with Kant's aesthetic theory. In an introductory essay to their new edition of the book, Christopher Landerer and Lee Rothfarb downplay the possibility of any direct influence, suggesting that what Kantianism there is in the text got there by way of cultural osmosis, as opposed to self-conscious adoption. Alexander Wilfing is even more emphatic, arguing that scholars who see the influence of the Third Critique in *OMB* have made a historical blunder.[8] He points out that state censorship guaranteed that the critical philosophy had little direct impact on Austrian scholars. In fact, Hanslick is unlikely to have familiarized himself with the details of Kant's aesthetics, so any reference to a 'Kantian framework' in his thought is either banal or misleading. Hanslick's real influences were a crew of lesser-known nineteenth-century

---

8   Wilfing 2018.

figures, such as Friedrich Theodor Vischer and Johann Friedrich Herbart. For Wilfing, understanding Kant as a source for Hanslick's aesthetic formalism is merely a bit of historical imprecision that has unfortunately solidified as conventional wisdom.

The answer to the historical question of Kant's influence, however, might be less instructive than the intuition that inspires it. This latter is less responsive to biographical than to broader, philosophical concerns. If, in light of the above, we read Hanslick's text as consequence and expression of political liberalisation, it is counterintuitive to look for those concerns solely in the Third Critique's discussion of reflective judgments of taste. That scope is altogether too narrow if what is ultimately at stake in the argument is the status of musical knowledge in an emergent post-autocratic society in general, and in its correspondingly reformed university in particular. Hanne Appelkvist identifies what she calls a 'Kantian ethos' in Hanslick's text, referring in particular to its 'conception of freedom as self-legislation'.[9] It is Kantian values, she suggests, not aesthetic doctrines that animate the argument. Along these lines, *OMB* can be read as extending the Copernican Turn to music, accomplishing for musical knowledge what Kant had for the physical and biological sciences.

There is, nevertheless, something apparently anachronistic in interpreting Hanslick in explicitly Kantian terms. The critical moment in philosophy preceded *OMB* by more than half a century. Confidence in Enlightenment rationalism had long been attenuated by philosophical romanticism. The work of Fichte, Schelling, and in particular Hegel, had decisively displaced the critical philosophy, preparing the way for novel departures such as Max Stirner's radical egoism and Ludwig Feuerbach's anthropological critique of religion. Further, if Kant's achievements were associated with the French Revolution, the political import of his thought could scarcely be considered contemporary after Thermidor, the 18th Brumaire, and Waterloo. All that said, Hanslick's Kantianism is only an anachronism if measured against the abstract progress of intellectual or political history. Picking up on a well-known formulation, concrete historical progress is, in actuality, geographically articulated, uneven and combined. In the context of Austria's political and institutional backwardness the anachronism disappears.

Consider that Kant himself helped lay the groundwork for university reforms that would be adopted first by the University of Berlin in the first half of the nineteenth century, and then by the University of Vienna after 1848. In his 1798 *The Conflict of the Faculties*, Kant addresses the need for freedom of teach-

---

9 Appelkvist 2011, p. 75.

ing and learning by defending the independence of the lower, philosophical faculty from undue encroachments from the higher, theological and professional faculties. The proximate occasion for the treatise was what Kant took to be undue interventions on the part of Königsberg's theological faculty in the work of philosophers since the death of Prussia's Enlightened monarch, Frederick the Great. Indeed, Prussian university administration had drifted so far to the right since Frederick's death that Kant's text was initially censored. When the treatise finally appeared, it served as a reference text for the university reform movement. The endeavour was a relatively pressing matter. At the turn of the nineteenth century, it was not clear that the university as such had a viable future. Specialized academies and technical schools appeared poised to render these medieval legacy institutions unable to carry out a social function.[10] In arguing for the importance of an independent philosophical faculty, Kant provided a framework for the continued relevance of the university as an institution. Given that in Vienna of the 1850s the conflict of the faculties was a living question, it is not surprising that Hanslick's attempt to carve out a place for musical science in the reformed university should be largely continuous with that Kantian framework.

At the centre of Kant's polemic is the relationship of reason to authority. 'It is absolutely essential', he writes:

> ... that the learned community at the university also contain a faculty that is independent of the government's command with regard to its teachings; one that, having no commands to give, is free to evaluate everything, and concerns itself with the interests of the sciences, that is, with truth: one in which reason is authorized to speak out publicly. For without a faculty of this kind, the truth would not come to light (and this would be to the government's own detriment); but reason is by its nature free and admits of no command to hold something as true (no imperative 'Believe!' But only a free 'I believe'). The reason why this faculty, despite its great prerogative (freedom), is called the lower faculty lies in human nature; for a man who can give commands, even though he is someone else's humble servant, is considered more distinguished than a free man who has no one under his command.[11]

Even through language carefully crafted to survive the scrutiny of censors, one can discern that Kant means modernity in university education to entail a

---

10   Bahti 1987, p. 438.
11   Kant 1979, p. 29.

reversal of the relations of dependence among the faculties. If it appeared that the lower faculty depends on the higher, which it serves, Kant reveals that it is the higher that depends on the lower, which grounds its access to truth. The lower gives no commands of itself, but rather serves to conduct the *sui generis* power of reason, what Jürgen Habermas calls an 'unforced force'.

The crux of the passage is the identification of the power of reason with the free 'I believe'. The individual subject is not wholly overcome by the commands of rulers or priests. In fact, the modern subject is distinguished by a self-grounding form of personal authority. Rulers and priests can and did command what was taught in the university classroom. Neither, however, can meaningfully command what can be held to be true. Holding something as true is a matter of modern, subjective authority. Kant allows for practical submission to the dictates of external authorities, but leaves no room for blind faith. Absent blind faith, the individual comes to be involved in establishing the authority of commands. For the modern subject, nothing can be authoritative unless taken to be so, freely believed. The work of reason serves to guarantee this freedom by identifying and tracking entailments and exclusions, and warding off contradiction. Contradiction threatens to render the contents of commands meaningless, thereby destroying the sovereignty of their source. That source need not be external. The commitment on the part of a commanding authority to the rational coherence of the content of its commands is the same as that of the subject in judgment with respect to the contents of what is judged. For Kant, in fact, that commitment just *is* subjectivity. Its capacity for moral action and judgement, the full scope of its authority, then, is rooted in reason. The unforced force of reason holds subjects responsible for the principled basis of their actions, as well as for what they can claim to know through experience.

Given that reason is the ground of its freedom, Kant's modern subject is a discursive entity. In order to count as pertaining to it, actions and experiences must be conceptually articulated. Nothing pre- or non-conceptual can get a genuine hold on an individual. Only the discursive can be integrated into subjective agency. Focused on the question of agency, Kant's concept of the concept is a normative one. Instead of understanding concepts as mental images, they are interpreted as rules. As the philosopher Robert Brandom reconstructs the view:

> Judging and acting, endorsing claims and maxims, committing ourselves as to what is or shall be true, is binding ourselves by norms – making ourselves subject to assessment according to rules that articulate the *contents* of those commitments. Those norms, those rules, he calls 'concepts'.

> In a strict sense, all a Kantian subject can do *is* apply concepts, either the-
> oretically, in judging, or practically, in acting. Discursive, that is to say,
> concept-mongering creatures, are normative creatures – creatures who
> live, and move, and have their being in a normative space.[12]

Kantian concepts are not psychic phenomena that may or may not relate to given worldly objects. Rather, they are rules that regulate how concepts relate to one another. Brandom calls these 'relations of compatibility and incompat-ibility'. The faculty of reason attends to these relations, while the active subject is free to apply concepts in judgment and action. The subject is normatively bound by the contents of the concepts deployed, but this binding is just the stuff of modern freedom.

In light of the above we can interpret Hanslick's project in *OMB* as a defense of the view that music is thoroughly discursive. This is to say that music making consists in deploying concepts. Of course, musical performances encompass activities that are transparently discursive, including and especially, the use of words. To make his point, then, Hanslick isolates aspects of musicianship that are not obviously conceptually articulate, namely, the 'purely' musical fea-tures of tonal structures. On this view, the relations of tones represent neither pre-verbal expressive utterances nor conformity to the physical demands of sounding bodies. Instead, they are moves in a space of reasons. This is what is at stake when Hanslick's insists that music making is thoroughly rational, akin to the conceptual moves in a Euclidian construction. 'Everything in [a tone] structure', he writes:

> ... is a spontaneous consequence and impact of the [main] theme, condi-
> tioned and shaped by it, dominated and fulfilled by it. It is the autonom-
> ous axiom that satisfies in the moment, but that our intellect wants to
> see contested and developed, as then occurs in the musical elaboration,
> analogous to a logical chain of reasoning.[13]

Hanslick maintains that in committing to a theme, the musician makes a move in a space of musical reasons. The listener's intellect, including that of the listening musician, is involved in relating subsequent moves to previous ones. Following Brandom, we can say that musical moves stand to one another in relations of compatibility and incompatibility. The content of a musical move

---

12   Brandom 2006, p. 7.
13   Hanslick 2018 [1854], p. 113.

consists in the full set of its entailments and exclusions. These are never all immediately obvious. If there is a desire on the part of the intellect to hear a theme developed, it is born of scepticism. As the music's course demonstrates how musical moves can be rationally related to one another, an ear sceptical of the musical potential of a given theme is naturally relieved, and perhaps even delighted, to hear and tacitly endorse unanticipated examples of musical soundness.

Having brought musical moves into the normative realm of the discursive, Hanslick characterizes the listener as actively involved in establishing rightness in music. Appropriately attending to music making necessarily involves judging, even if a listener is not aware of it. In his words:

> ... the [activity of] imagination, confronted with the beautiful, is of course not merely a *viewing*, but rather a viewing with understanding, that is, mental representation and judgment. The latter of course occurs with such speed that the individual processes do not even rise to consciousness, and the deception arises that something *unmediated* happens, which in reality depends on intellectual processes mediating in various ways.[14]

That mediation consists in the active deployment of concepts in judgement, an aspect of his position that is made especially perspicuous in Landerer and Rothfarb's new translation of the text's famous description of music's content as '*tönend bewegte Formen*'. Rather than render the phrase as 'sounding form in motion', or even as 'tonally moving forms', the latest translation settles on 'sonically moved forms', which hews closer to the grammar of the original. 'Sonically moved forms', they write, 'are thus forms that are moved in a way that can be heard'.[15] Previous translators might have shied away from the passive voice employed in the original. Indeed, taken on its own, the expression is unhelpfully vague about what force or agent does the moving. However, with the conditions for musical discursivity in mind, we can read the phrase as insisting on the subject's participation in the determinateness of sounding forms. These forms are conceptual insofar as they are moves in tonal space, the content of which encompasses any given move's compatibilities and incompatibilities, entailments and exclusions. Sonically moved forms are, then, articulate actions for which musician and listener can and should take responsibility.

---

14   Hanslick 2018 [1854], p. 5.
15   Hanslick 2018 [1854], p. xliii.

Hanslick's formalism is often read as an anxious attempt to preserve the purity of music from the threat of extra-musical significance. The polemical tone he frequently resorts to in *OMB* helps to recommend this reading. That said, the threat posed by extra-musical meaning is not to the ideology of musical purity, but to the determinateness of musical concepts. As Appelkvist makes the point:

> ... regulative rules derived from extramusical principles would [...] limit the freedom of composers as well as turn the understanding of music into an exercise of mechanically translating musical phrases into political dictums or emotional reports. But the musical grammar Hanslick talks about has little to do with such regulative prohibitions and obligations. There is no sanction for failure to follow the musical rules or for breaking them. Rather, the kinds of rules Hanslick refers to constitute the very musical system.[16]

If musical moves are mechanical translations of extra-musical concepts, they are not genuinely conceptual. The rightness of musical moves does not ultimately derive from their correspondence to non-musical conditions. Rightness is matter of musical grammar, the rationality of which corresponds to the conditions of the modern subject.

3   Against the Rule of Sentiment

While this conception of musical discursivity may strike the reader as an untimely addition to Enlightenment thought, it is important to note that Hanslick's views diverge significantly from the mainstream of eighteenth-century writing and thinking about music. Having recourse to a theoretical foil can be useful in clarifying the importance of Hanslick's intervention. In 1777, Johann Nikolaus Forkel began his *Über die Theorie der Musik*, an essay-length prolegomenon to his groundbreaking music historical studies, with the thought that 'in no other science or art has the need for certain rules and regulations been so much disputed and doubted as in music'.[17] Forkel distinguishes his position, in the first instance, from those who deny the importance of musical norms, maintaining that musical rightness is fully available to human

---

16   Appelkvist 2011, p. 80.
17   Forkel 1777, p. 3.

beings prior to conceptual regulation. He denies music's noble savagery by analogy, with the thought that the botanical gifts of nature do not make the gardener's work superfluous. Nature cannot be counted on to produce orderliness, regularity, and coherence on its own, and it is precisely music's well-regulated character that renders it useful and compelling. He presented his mature view eleven years later in his *Allgemeine Geschichte der Musik*, in which he writes that 'nature has scattered only isolated beauties in music as in all its works. It is the work of man to seek them out and to produce, through purposeful combination, new and more perfect creations than does nature itself'.[18]

Forkel's concerns are close to Hanslick's. Like the latter, the former is primarily interested in music's constitutive rules. Forkel establishes a theoretical understanding of musical norms that makes them amenable to scientific investigation. Once identified and catalogued, the full set of currently relevant musical norms could be made readily accessible. His project is quintessentially enlightened. Musical knowledge which would otherwise have to be gleaned from tutors and tradition could be transferred to the public sphere. In addition, the grounds for that knowledge no longer had to rest exclusively on external authorities. Forkel is sure that a reasoned investigation into the nature of music will yield insight into its conceptual architecture. Once this is discovered, the modern musician has the means for making rational musical progress. Forkel's ambitions are decidedly grand – indeed, the scope of his general history proved too vast for his resources and was never completed – yet he saw his own work as continuous with what he took to be the normal course of musical progress throughout history. Forkel took for granted that musical knowledge came through experience. That which had been discovered about its nature had come from long and careful attention to it on the part of our forebears. Modern science represented merely the latest phase of development.

Forkel is keen to discover the rules that regulate music, but unlike Hanslick, he assumes that these rules are grounded in nature. 'Rules or artistic principles', he writes:

> ... are based on the nature of the subject and on the nature of man. They are a necessary consequence of the style and manner in which all things of nature customarily develop out of one another. This gradual development of all forces of nature lies, indeed, open before the eyes of all men.[19]

---

18   Bosworth Powers 1995, p. 47.
19   Forkel 1777, p. 76.

The laws of nature may be available to mankind through observation, but this does not necessarily imply that those laws are authoritative. Musical rules can be grasped conceptually, but Forkel establishes their hold on us by assuming that there exists a general isomorphism between the relationships of tones to one another in music, on the one hand, and the relationships of feelings to one another in experience on the other. He expresses this isomorphism by referring to a 'language of sentiment'. 'All characteristics that create the perfect language of understanding on the one hand, also create similarly the perfect language of the heart on the other', he tells us.[20] On this view, feeling and knowing are twin faculties. Music is coherent because it represents a flow of feelings, and these hang together by virtue of a logic that is proper to them. Even tonal structures that appear expressively neutral derive their coherence from pre-conceptual somatic experience. He writes, for example, that 'double counterpoint is based, namely, on diverse modifications of feelings and on the true best use of the entire artistic wealth that nature offers for purposeful expression of those diverse feelings'.[21]

Forkel's name only appears twice in *OMB*, but his position on the role of feelings in determining the rightness of musical rules is precisely the one Hanslick polemicizes against. Hanslick does not assume a pre-established coordination of the logic of concepts with a supposed logic of feelings. Like Kant, he restricts the normative force of reason to the discursive realm. For writers like Forkel, 'works of music fall in line with *products of nature*, whose enjoyment can charm us but cannot compel us to think, compel us to ponder a consciously creative intellect'.[22] The hold that the products of nature have on us does not conform to the demands of the modern subject. Somatic experience can be powerful, even overpowering, and can result in pleasure. Those experiences, however, bypass subjective agency. Whether or not he was aware of it, Hanslick adopts Kant's locution when he calls these experiences 'pathological'.[23] From the perspective of *OMB*, Forkel's attempt to offer a successor to heteronomous, traditional authority in music is insufficiently enlightened. Sentiments take the place of rulers and priests in the licensing and prohibition of musical moves.

For all the Kantianism in *OMB*, Hanslick departs significantly from Kant's aesthetic theory. As discussed above, Kant held that judgements of taste are reflective judgements, not objective cognitions. Feelings are key to the process, as

---

20   Forkel 1777, p. 48.
21   Forkel 1777, p. 68.
22   Hanslick 2018 [1854], p. 83.
23   Hanslick 2018 [1854], p. 82.

it is precisely the feeling of pleasure taken in the free play of the faculties of imagination and understanding – that is, between the faculty that constructs representations and that which subsumes these under concepts – that makes for an experience of the beautiful. Kant's discussions of the fine arts, music included, address matters of taste and are not focused on questions of rightness and validity. Further, Kant does not break with what Hanslick calls 'the aesthetics of feeling'. Like Forkel, he interprets the coherence of tonal structures as grounded in the expression of sentiment. He notes that in speech, the tone one takes expresses the feelings that attend whatever is said. The tonal arts base themselves in the tones of speech, cultivating them for their own sake. What Samantha Martherne calls his 'expressive formalism' consists in the view that 'our appreciation of the formal structures of a piece of music must be guided by our appreciation of how those structures express affects'.[24]

What is radical in Hanslick's intervention into aesthetic theory is clarified when read against his eighteenth-century predecessors. His argument that music making is not a mechanical translation of feelings, but rather a set of conceptually determinate moves for which the musician can be held responsible and to account does not leave room for interpreting the deployment of musical concepts in performance as fundamentally distinct from the use of concepts in speech. In fact, his conception of the 'musically beautiful' is ultimately not an aesthetic theory at all. 'The exclusive activation of *understanding* through the beautiful', he writes, 'operates *logically* instead of aesthetically'.[25] He persists in using the word, but his conception of beauty is not continuous with that of Baumgarten or Kant. When Hanslick refers to beauty, he can only mean rightness, the valid use of musical concepts.

Hanslick concludes his history of concert life in Vienna by reminding his readers that the revolutionary events of 1848 had led to an improved and more dignified musical culture. In his words, it had sounded 'a new, deeper fundamental tone' [*einen neuen, tieferen Grundton*].[26] I have argued here that the musical formalism of *OMB* is a philosophical expression of the new, post-autocratic period in history Hanslick saw emerging. By arguing for the thoroughgoing discursivity of music making, Hanslick sought to modernize the subject's relationship to musical knowledge. Neither traditional authority, nor the requirements of nature could legitimately ground musical norms. Just after earning a degree in law in a time of significant democratic unrest among his peers, Hanslick concluded that musical legislation must be self-legislation. This

---

24   Martherne 2014, p. 134.
25   Hanslick 2018 [1854], p. 6.
26   Hanslick 1869, p. 433.

is the substance of the scientific character of musical research conducted on this basis, and the justification for its incorporation into the university system.

A university science of music is the product of a revolution, and thus came about in the context of pervasive historical self-consciousness. In his 1862 article on the Viennese premier of the *St. Matthew Passion*, Hanslick wrote that:

> ... in musical matters, the public appears, with every passing year, to acquire more of this historical sense, the most precious heritage of our time. It knows how to isolate the modern, individual tendencies and customs from the monuments of a great past, and if, now and then, it bruises its feelers, it no longer yields to the instinctive impulse to draw them in again.[27]

It is little wonder that the science of music that grew up in the wake of *OMB* would be a historical science. Formalism and its democratic impulse laid the foundation for the central theoretical concept of classical musicology: style.

---

27   Hanslick 1963, p. 101.

CHAPTER 5

Style Criticism and Historical Materialism

Although not original to musicology, the concept of style is nonetheless found-ational to the discipline. In the preface to his revised edition of Donald Grout's widely-used textbook, *A History of Western Music*, Claude Palisca writes that 'the history of music is primarily the history of musical style'.[1] Glen Haydon, addressing the relationship of music history to theory in the university cur-riculum, describes 'one of the main objectives of advanced graduate studies in music' as explaining 'in music-technical terms the stylistic factors that dis-tinguish the music of different periods and different composers. Work of this type has been subsumed under the rubric of style-criticism'.[2] Richard Crocker's music history textbook, which remains in print more than a half century after it first appeared, is simply called *A History of Musical Style*.[3] Arguing for introdu-cing style-criticism into high school music curricula, Maynard Anderson writes that:

> ... the varied, countless, and fascinating ways in which the parts [of music] can be arranged and interrelated result in that complex yet fundamental musical phenomenon – style. Musical style is a basic principle in the structure of the discipline of music.[4]

The writing of music history did not always demand use of the concept. The term itself in both German and English is a French borrowing that came into common usage in the eighteenth century.[5] In his 1789 *A General History of Music*, Charles Burney makes use of the term, but not in a systematic way. Bur-ney prefers to speak of the 'state' and 'progress' of music in various regions and at various times. R.G. Kiesewetter's *History of the Modern Music of West-ern Europe* – a title that can be misleading when one considers that for him musical modernity begins with the medieval Christian church – divides his material into periods he calls 'epochs'.[6] These are named for musicians (the

---

1 Grout and Palisca 1988, p. ix.
2 Haydon 1963, p. 250.
3 Crocker 1966.
4 Anderson 1966, p. 87.
5 Guido Adler was convinced that this occurred much earlier, in the fourteenth century.
6 Kiesewetter 1848, p. x.

list includes Hucbald and Guido d'Arezzo, Rossini and Beethoven) whose work is held to be definitive of each epoch. Kiesewetter recognized the need for a music historical concept that transcended the output and influence of individuals, but he did not go so far as to introduce a new theoretical concept. His approach, therefore, rests somewhere between a biographical method that dates back to Vasari's *Lives of the Artists* and scientific musicology. The theory of style in music was formally introduced and defended by Hanslick's successor at the University of Vienna, Guido Adler. The concept is the central theme of his 1911 *Style in Music* [*Der Stil in der Musik*] and its companion volume published eight years later, *Method of Music History* [*Methode der Musikgeschichte*]. It is Adler's conception of style that reappears with such frequency in subsequent musicology, sometimes explicitly, as in Knud Jeppesen's justly famous *The Style of Palestrina and the Dissonance*. For the most part, however, Adler's intervention goes unnoticed, having become disciplinary convention.

1   Style and Its Discontents

Despite being a foundational methodological principle, style criticism is not without its discontents. Reflecting on changing attitudes Allan Moore writes that:

> ... the operative distinctions between the terms 'style' and 'genre' seemed largely transparent during both my undergraduate and my postgraduate studies, a transparency which seemed to be of no great concern to my peers. Recently, however, it has appeared to me that the foundations of these apparent certainties were insecure.[7]

In fact, uncritical uses of the term are decidedly unwelcome and consequently rare in professional, English-speaking musicology today. As the editors of a recent collection of articles on biological approaches to the study of music note, 'any discussion of the evolution of musical styles throughout the world depends strongly on a theory of musical classification, and [...] this topic has been all but taboo in musicology'.[8] Indeed, Adler's many explicit references to the natural sciences make folding his music historical classifications into a broader narrative about the triumph of scientism in the late nineteenth

---

7   Moore 2001, p. 432.
8   Wallin, Merker, and Brown 2000, p. 19.

century a relatively straightforward matter. As we have already seen, Adler's reputation has fallen victim to the New Musicological historiography of the discipline and its inherited critique of scientific reason. One result of this has been that secondary literature on Adler routinely avoids any attempt to evaluate the content of his work. Most writers are primarily concerned to identify and criticize his ideological commitments, especially to categories native to the life sciences. That, for example, is precisely the subject of Benjamin Breuer's dissertation, 'The Birth of Musicology from the Spirit of Evolution: Ernst Haeckel's *Entwicklungslehre* as Central Component of Guido Adler's Methodology for Musicology'.[9] Excellently researched, Breuer's text nevertheless suspends judgement on the scholarly value of Adler's music historical theories so as to focus on his conceptual borrowings from evolutionary biology. Breuer interprets these borrowings as aspects of Adler's 'painting musicology as a science' so as to conform to late-nineteenth-century academic habits. Reduced to a moment in the dialectic of Enlightenment, Adler's style criticism is rendered impossible to engage with and evaluate on its own terms. Absent such engagement, his conception of style is subject to neither revision nor refutation. Rather, taboo and suspicion attach to the concept.

In a substantial article on Adler's style concept, Rachel Mundy endeavours to ground that suspicion by 'situating present usage within a historical arc spanning the racial theories of the 1930s, the soul-searching of the post-Holocaust period, and the aftershocks of the Cold War'. Those contexts are relevant because 'one of the core tools of music scholarship – the recognition and categorisation of musical style – is entangled in a historical tradition of categorising culture as a form of essential, biologized difference', the product of a 'racial imagination'.[10] The entanglement Mundy describes is especially pernicious because it operates behind the backs of those who employ the concept. However inspired he was by the methodology of the life sciences, Adler nowhere claims that musical style is a category of natural history. On the contrary, as Mundy points out, 'in many ways this new style-criticism made available a history of music that rejected racial politics by abstention, focusing musicological attention on music's formal elements instead of its national or ethnic features'. That new focus, however, only apparently rendered the concept free of its morally suspect biological implications. These remained in what Fredric Jameson might call the 'political unconscious' of a style-critical discourse that imagined itself to have won through formal-

---

9   Breuer 2011.
10   Mundy 2014, p. 738.

ism a noble immunity to partisanship. Mundy explicitly locates her decoding of the racialist logic always implicit in style criticism downstream of 'Kerman's admonition against science'.[11] She extends the critique of rationalisation to encompass the dehumanising conceptual architecture of that specifically biological strand of racism that underwrote the machinery of death at Auschwitz. She takes it that critical alertness to this degenerate use of reason is important because the same architecture persists in the form of speciesism today.

Mundy's argument lends moral justification to the discipline's turn away from style criticism. By identifying what she takes to be its ineliminably racialist logic, she aims to expose the method's implicit reactionary politics. While her argument proceeds by offering a series of historical contexts in which to interpret the musicological concept of style, none of these happens to involve Adler's express political convictions. This is an unfortunate omission, given that what can be known of these necessarily complicates Mundy's interpretive schema. From his youth Adler's politics were decidedly liberal. Far from endorsing 'biologized difference', he publicly supported the contemporary women's rights movement. As a law student, he proposed legislative reforms that would liberate women from the economic constraints involved in marriage contracts. His democratic ideals were not a symptom of youth. The Institute for Musicology Adler founded at the University of Vienna in 1898 broke with academic convention by counting women among its students. Especially troubling for Mundy's account is Adler's consistent and explicit opposition to national chauvinism. In reminiscences about his father, Adler's son writes:

> When my father became an assistant professor (Privatdozent) at the University of Vienna, and also during his Associate Professorship in Prague the clashes (on religious-racist grounds) with his 'Nordic' colleagues became worse and worse until they almost became intolerable during his tenure of full professorship in Vienna.[12]

Adler's enthusiastic support for Czech composers represented a significant enough rebuke to the nationalism of his colleagues at the German university in Prague that he initially felt obliged to attend performances of Czech opera in secret. Once his political liberalism became known, however, Thomas Garrick Masaryk, the future prime minister of Czechoslovakia, began attending Adler's lectures. On this matter, too, Adler appears to have maintained his position into

---

11   Mundy 2014, p. 759.

12   Quoted in Breuer 2011, p. 20.

later life. In 1925, at the age of seventy, he defended what he called 'internationalism in music', writing that:

> ... while nationalism directs its chief attention to the ascertainment of and insistence upon national qualities, with a tendency to racial narrowness, it is incumbent on internationalism to ascertain and set forth those artistic phenomena which are common property.[13]

Internationalism was, for Adler, not just a political imperative, but a scientific one as well. His massive music editorial project, *Denkmäler der Tonkunst in Österreich*, restricted itself to Austrian sources, not in order to privilege German culture, but because the project counted on financial backing from the Austrian state. Adler hoped that other European governments would support parallel endeavours with the sources to which their scholars could obtain direct access. As he was at pains to stress, musical organisation in Europe had taken on an international character since the Carolingian Empire at the latest. One notes that the monuments of tone art Adler collected were located in Austria, but not necessarily of it. Among the most significant sources Adler worked on was a set of seven manuscripts that preserve a largely French repertory of fifteenth-century polyphony, including important works by Dufay, known collectively as the Trent Codices after the city in which they were discovered. An Austrian edition of French music found in an Italian source exemplifies classical musicology's internationalism, which in this instance sought to make more readily available that which Adler considered 'common property'.

If Adler's obvious and sustained interest in the methods of the natural sciences is neither explained away with reference to his biography – Adler's presumed susceptibility to the intellectual fashions of his time – nor subjected to ideology critique, his methodological intervention can nonetheless be clarified in terms familiar from the previous chapter. Like Hanslick, Adler was primarily concerned to establish the authority of musical norms. The opening passage of his 'Scope' essay distinguishes between 'natural song [that] breaks forth from the throat freely and without reflection' and 'tonal art', which is organized and regulated by rules. Because musicology is, in the first instance, nothing but the process of making explicit to consciousness what these norms are and how they come to have the normative force and content that they do, musicology is as old as music making itself. The scope of that science is determined by 'the state of development of the tonal art'. Indeed, the question of what rules regu-

---

13   Adler 1925, p. 281.

late music is decidedly ancient. Euclid's *Division of the Monochord*, composed around 300 B.C.E., demonstrates the rational relations pitches in the Greek tone system stand in with respect to one another. The mathematical division of the monochord results in a collection of concepts – *mese, paramese*, etc. – that represent potential moves in musical space.[14] Expansion of the network of musical concepts entails proportionate expansion in musical capacities. These are not limited to tuning, but include rhythmic and harmonic concepts, as well as concepts that regulate the relationship of musical moves to those in other arts, such as dance and poetry. Music's rules constitute the art, and, as Adler points out, their being made explicit is routine in music history.

2   Style and Spirit

If musicology necessarily excludes 'natural song', then it follows that Adler's modelling musicology after the natural sciences does not stem from a commitment to naturalism. He is not identifying those forces external to human intentionality that determine the features of musical phenomena, as it were, from the outside. As many commentators have noted, he adopts key features of Hanslick's formalism, which, as we have seen, is intent on demonstrating the thoroughgoing discursivity of music making. Starting, then, from the premise that the subject is involved in the coherence and authority of musical concepts, Adler moves on to another, closely related concern. As he writes in *Style in Music*, 'even the boldest innovator is organically dependent on the prevailing sentiments [*Grundstimmung*] among his contemporaries if his art is to achieve a style character and a characteristic style of intrinsic value with significance for the progress of art'.[15] Given that musical moves are rational and not reflexive, they are the sorts of actions for which we can be held to account. The subject is involved in the determination of rightness in music, but not exclusively. The space of musical reasons in which the musician moves is always already in conceptual shape before the musician intervenes. Beginning from the assumption that musical moves are the sort of actions for which we can hold ourselves and one another responsible, Adler's focus turns to what musicians are responsible *to* when they make such moves. Hanslick asked after the form of musical concepts, their capacity for being rationally articulated to one another, while Adler is concerned with their content, that is, with the precise concepts involved.

---

14   Mathiesen 1975.
15   Adler 1911, p. 6.

By way of motivating this shift, Adler refers to Richard Wagner's *The Art-work of the Future*. The text was familiar to him, not only due to its widespread literary influence, but also because Adler had been involved in advocacy for Wagner's music dramatic project since his student days. He met the composer at Wahnfried on a pilgrimage to Bayreuth in the company of Bruckner as a young man, an episode he describes at length in his autobiography. He sustained his interest in the composer into later life, eventually publishing a book-length study of Wagner's stylistic development in 1904.[16] In *Style*, Adler argues that whatever features the artwork of the future might have in theory, any realized artwork cannot represent an absolute break with the present. Indeed, Wagner's own attempts to deliver on his literary promises were inevitably created for contemporaries and responsive to their expectations. Whatever technical innovations the composer is celebrated for pioneering ultimately derived their authority not from novelty or originality, but from the latent possibilities afforded by a musical grammar already up and running. Progress in music involves generating new musical concepts or extending the entailments of established concepts. Nevertheless, neither can be intelligible in abstraction from a background of shared commitments. While it may spring from the creativity of an individual, no technical novelty can count as having expanded or altered music's discursive vocabulary without eventually establishing itself as authoritative in a relevant community of music makers.

While Adler does not discuss it, Wagner himself took up this theme in *Art-work*. Like his fellow Young Hegelians, Wagner accepted Hegel's critique of Kant's formal, subject-centred conception of reason. Hegel observed that any given intentional action divides itself in two in the process of being done. In the language he employs in the *Phenomenology of Spirit*, there is a distinction between an action [*Handlung*] on the one hand, and the deed [*Tat*] accomplished through the action on the other. The moment of action is determined by the agent, while the moment of the deed is what the action means for others. Hegel stresses the two-fold character of intentional action in response to Kant's efforts to ground the universal authority of judgments and moral actions in the conditions of subjectivity alone. Because Kant understood the subject to be constituted by the unity of its rational commitments, the rightness of actions could be guaranteed by their following from a maxim that could be adopted universally without thereby becoming meaninglessly contradictory. This is the substance of his 'categorical imperative'. On this view, contradiction-eliminating subjectivity could serve as the sole basis for rightness in action.

---

16   Adler 1904.

Putting this in musical terms, a string player has a rational duty to play in tune. Absenting this maxim threatens to render the meaning of intonation obscure. However, what counts as being in tune for one might not so count for another. Following this maxim does not necessarily determine anything about the musical result. Reason alone cannot decide between claims and therefore cannot serve as a universal basis for determining rightness in the use of a musical concept.

Hegel's suggested alternative basis is what he calls 'spirit'. Few philosophical terms have been so variously interpreted. This is at least in part due to Hegel's manner of expression. A recent English approximation to his own inimitable prose has it that:

> ... as ethical substance and abiding essence, all-encompassing and self-concordant, spirit is the imperturbable, indissoluble ground and point of departure for the activity of everyone; and as the neotic [*gedachte*] inner principle of all self-conscious beings, it is their common purpose and goal.[17]

Many readers understand Hegel to be making a metaphysical, even a mystical argument. The philosopher Charles Taylor, for example, identifies Hegel's spirit concept with God. 'The universe is posited as the conditions of existence of God or *Geist*', he writes. As such, it is 'the embodiment of the totality of the "life-functions" of God [...] and it also is throughout an expression of God, that is, something posited by God in order to manifest what he is'.[18] The tradition of emphasising the theological aspects of Hegel's concept, however, enjoys relatively little influence in English-language philosophy today. Exegetical work by Robert Pippin and Terry Pinkard published in the late 80s and early 90s set the stage for a reinterpretation of Hegel characterized by an understanding of 'spirit' as what Pinkard calls 'the sociality of reason'. Before the French Revolution and Kant's critical philosophy had birthed modern self-consciousness and the attendant demand that the meaning of all actions originate in the subject, the inherent sociality of reason could only be in itself, not for itself. It is only when the modern subject attempts to ground its authority in abstraction from external conditions that the nature of its dependence on others is made plain to it in experience. The premodern subject experienced this dependence as fate. Free from transgressive intentions, Sophocles' Oedipus is nonetheless respons-

---

17   Hegel 2019 [1807], p. 216.
18   Taylor 1977, p. 88.

ible for the meaning his actions have for others. In Hegel's terms, he is responsible for his deeds, and not just his actions. The shape of spirit that reigned in
Ancient Greece and which regulated the meaning of actions in that society ran
roughshod over the intentions of individuals. Antigone, for example, is put to
death for an action that would count as an act of conscience in the modern
world. Writing in the midst of profound transformations in European politics,
Hegel stressed that the shape of spirit that was emerging with the nineteenth
century would not only have to leave room for subjective intentions, but underwrite their legitimacy. The modern spiritual community, then, is a society of
individuals who mutually recognize each other as authoritative subjects. The
individual derives his free subjectivity precisely from his dependence on others
who collectively grant it.

From the first, this notion of spirit was not merely a bit of speculative philosophy. There was political import to Hegel's argument. The historical shape
of spirit Hegel thought necessary to meet the individual's demand for subjective authority would have to rely upon the mediation of social institutions.
The sociality of reason does not reside in a metaphysical realm of things-in-
themselves, but rather becomes manifest in the structure of the family, civil
society, and the state. As John Toews has argued, Hegel's critique of Kant's
abstract conception of subjective authority was fit to the political circumstances of his time.[19] He was born into a family with close connections to
the Württemberg ducal court, which, like many such courts in Germany in
the second half of the eighteenth century, was intent on taking on the centralising functions of a modern state, a process that involved appropriating
and endorsing Enlightenment ideology. In the case of Württemberg the local
nobility enjoyed relatively more power than, for example, their Prussian counterparts, and thus ducal reforms were met with inordinate resistance from
those whose inherited privileges were at risk of being removed. While Hegel
responded with enthusiasm to the achievements of the French Revolution,
and even before the turn of the century had clearly sided with the modern
state building project and its Enlightenment, he was nonetheless fully aware of
the obstacles political modernity faced in Germany. After the Napoleonic inva-
sions, the modernising project was naturally associated with the French occupation, leading many educated Germans to embrace nationalism and philosophical romanticism. Hegel developed his system in response to both the
centralising rationalism that had arrived on horseback across the Rhine and
the conservative romanticism that attracted so many of his compatriots. The

---

19   Toews 1985.

circle could be squared if the socially constructed and historically constituted communal norms that romanticism sought to preserve by limiting the universalising demands of reason could be shown to have been emerged out of a rational developmental process. The substance of an ethical community, which Romantics like F.W.J. Schelling had thought available to consciousness only through non-rational means, especially aesthetic experience, could in Hegel's estimation be brought fully under concepts. Once the inherent rationality of social norms and institutions had become the property of all by virtue of their having become the object of science, their hold on the individual would no longer come into conflict with the necessary conditions of subjective agency and freedom.

The appeal of Hegel's conception of spirit for many of his contemporaries was severely limited by its association with the Prussian state. In 1818, Hegel accepted a position at the University of Berlin, an appointment designed explicitly to ally his project of bringing spirit to self-consciousness with the existing Prussian bureaucracy. In selecting Hegel, state officials sought to lend philosophical legitimacy to their reconstruction efforts in the wake of the Napoleonic Wars. For Hegel, the position represented an invaluable chance to make his system, in principle the property of all, available to the widest possible audience from the centre of what he deemed to be Germany's most progressive state. By the 1820s, however, the contrast between the Hegelian promise of a self-conscious ethical community of free individuals who maintain and foster each other's subjective freedom, on the one hand, and the reality of Prussian politics on the other had become too stark to ignore. Nevertheless, Hegel's influence among German academics and intellectuals did not diminish as a result of this tension between philosophy and reality. In fact, those who had found their way to his brand of 'absolute idealism' experienced their acceptance of his doctrine as a quasi-religious conversion. Rather, those who came to be known as 'Left Hegelians' reacted by innovating within the system they inherited. With enthusiasm for centralising state projects having faded for many, the goal of philosophy shifted to directing action. As Marx famously put it in his *Theses on Feuerbach*, 'the philosophers have only interpreted the world, in various ways; the point is to change it'.[20]

Along with this change in emphasis from rational justification to revolutionary zeal, Hegelianism in the period around 1848 frequently abandoned key elements of the deceased master's system. Among the suppressed elements were the critique of nationalist enthusiasm and, importantly, the denial that aes-

---

20   Marx 1992, p. 423.

thetic experience had any longer a meaningful part to play in society's maturity. This latter, Hegel's 'end of art' thesis, was particular unpopular. As Toews puts it:

> ... the claim that the content of art [...] could be fully translated, without any loss of content, into the conceptual language of reason, that the absolute ultimately found a language adequate to its content in the conceptual terms of Hegelese was, for many contemporaries, the most striking and irritatingly pretentious manifestation of the Hegelian position.[21]

Written in the same period as *OMB*, but in significantly different circumstances, Wagner's *Artwork* exemplifies these features of Left Hegelian literature. It was Wagner's explicit intention that the book be read as a contribution to post-Hegel Hegelianism. The book's title, for example, is a reference to Ludwig Feuerbach's 1843 *Principles of the Philosophy of the Future*. In addition, Wagner adopted the Left Hegelian anthropological variation on Hegel's developmental, historicist theme. Rather than tracing the Idea as it made itself known in worldly history, Wagner followed Feuerbach in substituting Man for a conception of self-objectifying mindedness. This anthropological turn in Wagner's text is joined to romantic assumptions about *Volk* and nation. Because he heartily embraces revolutionary politics, placing the resolution of subject and society in an ideal future, Wagner's is a Left Hegelianism. His progressive nationalist politics, however, are mobilized in the service of aesthetic experience. The former is understood to be the condition for the full flowering of the latter. He oscillates between predicting the rise, and calling for the establishment of 'the free Artistic Fellowship'. This revolutionary social form constitutes:

> ... the foundation, and the first condition, of the Artwork itself. From it proceeds the Performer, who, in his enthusiasm for this one particular hero whose nature harmonizes with his own, now raises himself to the rank of Poet, of artistic Lawgiver to the fellowship; from this height, again, to descend to complete absorption in the fellowship. The function of this lawgiver is therefore never more than periodic, and is confined to the one particular occasion which has been prompted by his individuality and thereby raised to a common 'objective' for the art of all; wherefore his rule can by no means be extended to all occasions.[22]

---

21   Toews 1993, p. 385.
22   Wagner 1993.

In Wagner's utopian future, those artists whose personal intuitions happen to be calibrated to meet the general aesthetic needs of society thereby acquire universal authority, an acquisition that fades as soon as the fit between the individual's personal style and the style required by society no longer holds.

3   Style and Technique

In working out his own formulation of the problem of the universality of the modern musician's subjective authority, Adler drew upon Wagner's theoretical legacy while rejecting its nationalistic utopianism. His monograph on the composer takes the position that Wagner's extravagant philosophy of art does not even serve as a useful interpretive key to his own works. All the same, Adler retains the Left Hegelian framework for understanding the problem and its stakes, as well as a materialist dissatisfaction with 'absolute' idealism. For a more satisfactory approach along these lines, Adler turned to the work of one of Wagner's contemporaries, the architect and art historian Gottfried Semper. Indeed, the opening sentence of *Style in Music* is a quotation from Semper, whose most influential text is a voluminous tome which appeared between 1860 and 1863 under the title *Style in the Technical and Tectonic Arts, Or, Practical Aesthetics*.[23] Born in 1803, Semper trained in Munich before finding himself in Paris during the July Revolution. By the time he was recruited to the Saxon court at Dresden a few years later, the architect had long been committed to radical republicanism. When the Dresden uprising broke out in 1848, Semper lent his skills to the struggle by advising in the design and fortification of street barricades. Wagner met Semper soon after his arrival in Dresden in 1842 and the two men built a lifelong friendship on the basis of shared cultural and political convictions. Due to their involvement in the uprising, warrants were issued for their arrest. Had they not fled the city, it is likely that neither would have survived custody. Semper remained close to Wagner and his artistic projects for decades thereafter, directly influencing the plan for the festival theatre in Bayreuth.

While Wagner had been concerned with the issue of style, it was Semper who made it the centrepiece of his thought. As a result, it is his conception of style that Adler adopted. This conception was partly the consequence of Semper's choice of where to settle in exile. Wagner had gone south to Switzerland, a state where political freedoms persisted as a result of relative economic under-

_____

23   Semper 2004 [1860].

development. By contrast, in 1851 Semper found himself in London, the centre
of global capitalism, where he attended the Great Industrial Exhibition. He had
already begun to develop a distinctive position on the history of architecture,
but his experiences in England impressed upon him the need for an approach
to art history that could interpret and react to the advent of industrial production. In his essay on the Exhibition, 'Science, Industry, and Art', he observes that
'it is already evident that inventions are no longer, as before, a means for avert-
ing privation and for enjoyment. On the contrary, privation and enjoyment
create the market for the inventions. The order of things as been reversed'.[24]
This point about the reversal of means and ends in production for the market
is strongly reminiscent of Marx whose analyses of the dynamics of capitalist
production frequently take the form of a dialectical opposition. This is hardly
a coincidence. Semper was fifteen years Marx's senior, but both men were
strongly influenced by idealist university philosophy in their youth while taking
political inspiration from revolutionary processes in France. Both fled political
repression in Germany and spent time in Paris before settling more permanently in London. In fact, both Semper and Marx worked on their respective
masterpieces in the library of the British Museum in the same period.

    Like Marx, Semper was at once enthused by the promise of industrial devel-
opment and a critic of its capitalist organisation. Replying to the suggestion
that financial speculation will 'seek out the best forces and acquire them for
itself', and for that reason show more discernment as an arts patron than 'a
Maecenas or a Medici', Semper writes that:

> ... in working for speculation man is doubly dependent: he is a slave to
> his employer and to the latest fashion that provides the employer with a
> market for his wares. Man sacrifices his individuality [...] for a pottage of
> lentils.[25]

Semper hones in on the alienation of product from producer that results as
craft production gives way to a more fine-grained division of labour. For neither
theorist does the market represent a satisfactory institution for mediating individual ends and those of society. Modern 'spirit', the sociality of reason in
advanced industrial society, does not appear as such, but instead takes the form
of a quasi-natural force that rules over individuals. The result is a 'Babylonian'
confusion, which does not allow the modern artist to make reasoned decisions

---

24   Semper 2004 [1860], pp. 133–4.
25   Semper 2004 [1860], pp. 139.

about how to go about producing. The purpose of Semper's style history is to disabuse industrial society of this confusion by revealing the rational order that lies underneath the trajectory of productive development. 'Were the world not fully occupied with its internal contradictions', he writes, 'external restraints (whatever they may be) would surely be unable to impede its development. The shackles would fall by themselves if the urge that drives the present became more generally aware of its aim'.[26] Note that it is the force that 'drives the present' that Semper anticipates will come to self-consciousness. His style history is a science of invention and it is precisely this human inventive capacity that has become the motive force in history. Once what is malign in production driven by speculation and exclusively for the market – what Marx calls its 'capitalist integument' – is driven away with the aid of rational insight, human invention can begin a period of ordered development.

Given this focus on invention, the development of technique is the keystone of Semper's project. Something of what Marx hoped would come of a Vichian history of technology can be observed here.[27] Semper's concern is with the arts, but these are understood to include the weaving of baskets and the manufacture of gas lamps. The whole of human making stands to be transformed by stylistic self-consciousness as the creative projects of individuals are knowingly reconciled to the requirements of time, place, and the trajectory of history. In Hegel, this reconciliation was, to be sure, mediated by worldly engagement, but ultimately occurs on an ideal plane. It is mindedness as such, spirit, that comes to self-consciousness, overcoming the sources of scepticism and allowing the subject to feel at home in what it nonetheless knows is a constructed world. Wagner insisted that the fine arts necessarily mediate this process. He is therefore focused on the necessary conditions for bringing about the 'artwork of the future'. In the first instance, these are political conditions, given that the freedom of each to rise to the level of poet-hero is what guarantees the freedom of all to achieve spiritual progress. Semper agrees that the arts play a mediating role, but extends the thesis to encompass the full range of creative production. It is no longer artistic achievement that leads to the satisfaction of mindedness, but scientific achievement that allows for the free development of the arts. That achievement is, in fact, sign and symptom of a communal stage of creative development.

Adler follows Semper in turning to material and technique. He writes that 'the crux of an art style lies in the selection of materials and the way they

---

26   Semper 2004 [1860], p. 130.

27   Marx 1976 [1867], p. 493.

are used', and further that 'technology [Teknik] is style-forming', indeed, it 'co-generates' an artwork.[28] Musical material does not arrive ready-to-hand, but results from the incomplete working up of musical ideas. Because 'every work of art is based on a motif or theme or several of them', they represent the 'starting point, the driving force behind every style'.[29] The technical affordances of formal elements serve as reasons for action. The process of music making itself generates new affordances, which in turn serve as reasons for further development. Reconstructing this process is at the heart of Adler's conception of music-historical work. He writes that:

> ... the most satisfying task of the scholar of art is to demonstrate and establish how, proceeding from the beginnings of simple melody, the structure of works of art gradually grows; how, proceeding from the simplest thesis, the artistic norms latent in the tonal products become more and more complicated; how tonal systems pass away with disappearing cultures; how, little by little, a chain of cells attaches itself to a limb and grows organically; how elements standing outside the mainstream of progressive development perish because they are not viable. One can say that the laws of art change with the generations; as manifold as the changes are, art attains different stages which, with reference to the beauty attainable within their limitations, cannot be overstepped.[30]

Adler's use of the term 'beauty' in the quoted passage is downstream of Hanslick's conceptual, if not terminological, break with the categories of philosophical aesthetics. Because it is subject to historical transformation, this notion of beauty is not Kant's. Because it is unconcerned with communal mindedness in its quest to become self-conscious, it is also not Hegel's. Following Semper, Adler's conception of beauty is restricted to describing the rightness a musical form can acquire at a given moment in the history of its grammar. He writes that:

> ... the style of an era, a school, an artist or a work can be viewed and investigated independently of the accompanying conception of beauty, and it is precisely the historian's responsibility to place himself outside the conception of beauty of his time.[31]

---

28   Adler 1911, p. 49.
29   Adler 1911, p. 50.
30   Mugglestone 1981, p. 8.
31   Mugglestone 1981, p. 11.

This understanding of beauty, along with the musicological project it allows to get up and running, presents itself as alternative and successor to an aesthetics of music. Interpreted in the context of the social and intellectual conditions of its emergence, style criticism's principal achievement can be said to lie in offering the modern musician a basis for evaluating musical moves that is based neither on individual taste, nor on the demands of mere convention. Style mediates between the individual and the social by determining the scope of subjective agency, as well as serving as its ground. A science of style is meant to offer the musician a means of inheriting and endorsing music's constitutive concepts that overcomes the modern forms of scepticism.

Of course, it is precisely this eschewal of the philosophical conception of beauty in favour of a teleological science of history that evokes the most serious scepticism in musicology today. Particularly disturbing are moments when Adler appears to make no distinction between musical and natural history. He asserts, for example, that 'the art of music is an organism, [composed of] a plurality of individual organisms which, in their interrelationships and interdependence, form a whole'.[32] Because this conflation is patently unwarranted, Adler's readers have largely dismissed his organicism as an impediment to genuine musical knowledge. However, if it is the case, as I have argued above, that Adler rejects naturalism, then the substance of his organicism must lie elsewhere. When Adler states that music is an organism composed of organisms, his point is about the relations musical concepts can and ought to stand in with respect to one another. In conjugating two musical concepts, the musician need not understand either to be the cause of the other. Instead, the coherence of individual musical moves depends on their being constitutive parts of a larger whole. This relation of part-to-whole is the same one that natural science since Aristotle has postulated regulates living organisms. Fin and gill are separate and distinct, but each stand as parts to the fish as a whole. Further, Adler's organicism implies that a unifying tendency toward some end or state explains the special tightness that characterizes this part-to-whole relation. Fin and gill are as they are because they contribute to a general tendency on the part of both the individual salmon or halibut, as well as their respective species, to stay alive and to thrive. Similarly, the moves that make up a given musical improvisation or composition (real or tonal answer, consequent phrase, authentic cadence) are as they are because they contribute to the tendency on the part of performances and compositions toward coherence and euphony. In insisting on organic relatedness, Adler is not merely borrowing a methodology from a

---

32   Adler 1911, p. 13.

natural science and grafting it onto the study of music. He is, rather, introducing a working hypothesis about how musical concepts tend to relate to one another.

Teleological explanation is important not just to Adler's understanding of individual works, but, more significantly for our purposes, to his theory of style. He writes that:

> ... the style of an epoch, a school, an artist, a work does not come about by chance, as a mere chance expression of the will to art it contains, but is based on the laws of becoming, of the ascent and descent of organic development.[33]

The teleological purposiveness that Adler finds at work in the history of tonal art need not imply that the course of music history follows a pre-established plan, or that its future can be predicted in advance. If one allows that music history has an end, that end need not be finite. Kant theorized that the judging subject requires the experience of what he called 'purposiveness without a purpose' in order to make both objective knowledge and responsible actions intelligible. The world must appear as if amenable to human ends, or else our conceptual grip on objects can be little more than arbitrary. As Rachel Zuckert summarizes the view, 'Kant's concept of purposiveness without a purpose is teleology not in the sense of *serving* a previously identified good, but of aiming *towards* an indeterminate future end, and this new form of teleology characterizes only and specifically human, judging subjects'.[34] For Kant, scientific knowledge cannot get going unless that which is under investigation is, in principle, understood to be open to subjective judgment. Hegel, extending Kant's subjective idealism into an absolute idealism, denies that teleology is restricted to judging subjects. Since it is collective mindedness, spirit itself, that is embodied in the world, its knowability is taken for granted. On Hegel's view, objectivity is a wholly product of human ends. Following Hegel, but breaking with his idealism, Semper and Marx identify human labour as the basis of our experience of purposiveness. The world is not, as Hegel thought, a product of mind, but of human hands. It is amenable to human ends because it is always already constructed. In his *Theses on Feuerbach*, Marx complains that Feuerbach only partially rejected Hegel's outlook. 'Feuerbach', he writes, 'not satisfied with abstract thinking, wants contemplation; but he does not conceive sensuousness as prac-

---

33   Adler 1911, p. 13.
34   Zuckert 2010, p. 10.

tical, human-sensuous activity'.[35] Since it is human activity that determines the sensible world, it is hardly surprising that the subject has an experience of teleology. And, indeed, it is precisely teleology and organicism that underwrite a scientific understanding of history.

4   Style and Historical Materialism

Even while it displays organic coherence, music before musicology necessarily developed largely unconsciously. To paraphrase Marx, the emergence of a science of style promises to bring music's prehistory to a close. Armed with a basis for evaluating interventions in the history of musical grammar, the modern musician can aspire to construct a 'music of the future' without having to take on a series of idealistic and ultimately intolerable Wagnerian presuppositions. That promise, however, was not to come to fulfilment. As late as 1939, the musicologist Warren Dwight Allen could complain that the discipline 'has not yet formulated a general *method*, a philosophy with reference to the whole field. One of the leaders, Guido Adler, will be quoted for his treatise on 'Method in Music History', but this turns out to be merely a discussion of *techniques* of style-criticism and identification'.[36] While Allen is an unsympathetic reader of Adler, he is nevertheless right in pointing out a significant gap in Adler's style-critical method. Once the scholar has gathered together the sources and identified relevant stylistic parameters, the question of what propels music history forward remains open. The focus on technique that Adler borrows from Semper and develops in *Style* can – and was – taken to be the basis for a *Geistesgeschichte*. Having identified technical development, the musicologist is then free to interpret change as a reflection of a broader cultural process of maturation. Pamela Potter has tracked the growth of both Neo-Kantian and Diltheyian approaches to the discipline during the period of the Weimar Republic.[37] Both tendencies represent a reaction against the materialist, organicist orientation of Adlerian style criticism. Both the Neo-Kantians and the *Geistesgeschichter* sought to preserve music's special status as a fine art, looking beyond the technical facts of its history to discover aesthetic and symbolic meaning. In a similar vein, Knud Jeppesen, once a student of Adler's, came to the view that music history is a reflection of psychology. He claims that:

---

35   Marx 1992, p. 422.
36   Allen 1939, p. xi.
37   Potter 1998.

... the background against which [the task of the music historian] should be considered is of a psychological nature, viz: the projection of the human into the musical. The way to the solution of this problem leads from without inward, seeking behind the notes upon the page their deeper psychological contents.[38]

It is an intriguing tack, one that replaces an idealistic notion of *Geist* with the *Geist* of modern psychology. It also serves as tacit acknowledgement of Allen's complaint that the classical conception of style remains under-theorized.

It is here that historical materialism is in a good position to make a meaningful contribution to musicology. Marx and Engels begin with the insight that meeting human needs, both individual and collective, takes work, the sacrifice of mind and muscle in productive life. Given that only the minor part of our individual needs can be met through our own efforts, everyone necessarily relies on the work of others. In history, people have distributed and controlled the work they do to meet collective needs in a variety of ways. These, however, are not selected arbitrarily, but tend to be suited to the productive capabilities, both qualitative and quantitative, a given society possesses at any given moment in its history. Marx and Engels presume that a tendency toward improvement and expansion is in the nature of the human productive capacity. As Marx puts it in the first volume of *Capital*:

A spider conducts operations which resemble those of the weaver, and a bee would put many a human architect to shame by the construction of its honeycomb cells. But what distinguishes the worst architect from the best of bees is that the architect builds the cell in his mind before he constructs it in wax. A the end of every labor process, a result emerges which had already been conceived by the worker at the beginning, hence already existed ideally. Man not only effects a change of form in the materials of nature; he also realizes his own purpose in those materials.[39]

This process of ideation and transformation separates human labour from the instinctual labour the beaver engages in when building a dam. Since both the process of labour and the purpose realized through labour are subject to change, there is every reason to expect a secular tendency toward sophistication, efficiency, and expansion, no matter what form human labour takes.

---

38   Jeppesen 1970, p. 8.
39   Marx 1976 [1867], p. 284.

This process, namely, the development of a society's productive forces, is the motive force in history. It is ultimately these capacities that lend credible normative force to the relations labourers stand in with respect to one another in the labour process. Control and responsibility, as aspects of work, underwrite less-concrete notions of right and duty. These latter can, then, be said to be superstructural with respect to the practical realities they rely on for their intelligibility. As society's productive forces develop, they strain the norms that govern social relations by offering up genuine possibilities for change.

If we take this approach to be valid for human labour in general, it follows that any particular field of productive life should lend itself to it equally well. Music making is just such a field. Many of our musical needs can be met through individual effort. Humming a lullaby, singing a birthday greeting, and serenading a lover can all be accomplished absent interpersonal collaboration, and with little or no formal training. More elaborate music, however, requires greater forces. A single melodic line can be embellished with contrapuntal lines above or below, or accompanied by a drone or other instrument. This is best accomplished through a division of labour. As musical capacities expand, so do these divisions. The labour of the keyboardist, for example, is eventually divided from that of the composer and that of the instrument's tuner. As the size of the standard orchestra expands, there is a tendency toward ever greater specialisation. Eventually a professional conductor comes to play a standard role. These divisions imply an uneven distribution of control over the musical making process as a whole. The historical materialist approaches music with the assumption that, because music making involves conscious productive activity, the relations musicians stand into with respect to one another is determined by the level of technology available to musicians at any given time.

Hanslick would agree with the historical materialist in insisting that music making is thoroughly discursive, and that this is the basis for its historicity. However, where Hanslick's treatise lacked an explanation for how musical forms acquire legitimacy, the materialist, having fully abandoned the idealist ambition to see in the fine arts a reflection of a spiritual reality, however broadly conceived, need only point to the relative efficiency and effectiveness of any given formal structure. On this view, the telos of music history is understood to be the production of broadly useful music in ever greater quantity and involving the fewest demands on the musician's time, brain, and muscle. A materialist conception of music history can also serve as a basis for understanding how music's formal structures appear to gather together in distinct styles, the borders of which are temporal, geographical, and, at times, personal. Music's productive forces develop unevenly, and can be held in check by any number of historical contingencies. Finally, they are, like those in all other economic sectors, tied to and conditioned by the development of economic forces in society as a whole.

It is by virtue of being so tied that there is a political edge to adopting a materialist conception of music history. In the 1859 *Preface*, Marx writes that 'at a certain stage of development, the material productive forces of society come into conflict with the existing relations of production. [...] Then begins an era of social revolution'. The existence of social relations that involve economic exploitation entails a constant struggle of the exploited against their conditions, and a constant defensive battle on the part of exploiters to maintain their position. Indeed, Marx and Engels famously note that 'the history of all society up to now is the history of class struggles'. However, it is only at a moment when the material conditions of production have grown, and thereby sufficiently changed so as to make inappropriate reigning relations of control and responsibility, that those relations lose their ability to reproduce themselves and legitimize both abstract ethical norms and laws. 'No social order', Marx writes:

> ... is ever destroyed before all the productive forces for which it is sufficient have been developed, and new superior relations of production never replace older ones before the material conditions for their existence have matured within the framework of the old society.

Adopting a materialist conception of history is only relevant in the context of the destruction of a social order and its conscious and intentional replacement by planned production under the control of a broad-based democratic regime. Both the destruction and the replacement of the social order require grounding in a science of history if those charged by historical contingencies to carry out the actions necessary for their success are to overcome scepticism about their meaning and appropriateness.

It was doubtless resistance to this political edge that prevented Adler himself from seeing and making good on the possibility for the productive synthesis of musicology and historical materialism. The father of the discipline remained a political liberal all his life, even after those nineteenth-century convictions had become decidedly anachronistic. In fact, the period of the development of university musicology is roughly coterminous with the period encompassing the rise of European Social Democracy as a mass movement, especially in Central Europe, and the first flowering of Marxist intellectual culture. There was scarcely a field of research that the Marxist theoretical press did not tackle between the Gotha Congress in 1875 and the German Revolution of 1918. August

Bebel had made serious materialist contributions to anthropology as early as 1879 in his classic *Woman and Socialism*. Engels would follow up on these with his *Origin of the Family, Private Property and the State* in 1884. In France, Jean Jaurès's 1901 *A Socialist History of the French Revolution* established the basic materialist premises for what would become the mainstream in historiography of that event through to the 1970s. Albert Mathiez, an outspoken Communist and supporter of the Bolsheviks, held the chair in the history of the revolution at the Sorbonne. Karl Kautsky, editor of the leading theoretical organ of German Socialism, *Die Neue Zeit*, published the results of his research on a vast array of subjects, including the history of Christianity and ethics. We have already seen that Marxists in the Second International period wrote extensively about the arts, especially literature. After the publication of the second and third volumes of *Capital* – 1885 and 1894 respectively – bourgeois economists felt compelled to react to Marx's value theory. Some bourgeois sociologists, such as Werner Sombart, were drawn into the orbit of Marxism by virtue of its explanatory power. Marx himself did not understand his project as hemmed in by disciplinary boundaries. While he never published it, he prepared a manuscript developing an alternative foundation for the calculus, one that would be theoretically consistent with his general materialist outlook. Boris Hessen and Henryk Grossmann would go on to apply historical materialism to the history of the natural sciences. For the scholar attracted to social democracy, there was ample opportunity for pursuing a Marxist line, no matter what the discipline. Had the first generation of university musicologists been persuaded by the intellectual arm of the workers movement, they would have found both readership and opportunities to publish.

If Social Democracy won few adherents among musicologists, this was not for lack of musician recruits to the movement. In fact, as already discussed, music permeated German socialism. Adler surely would have known of workers choruses and orchestras. Musicians had already begun to join labour unions, and the demonstrated success of the Marxist SPD relative to any other organized workers movement in history posed a pressing question for the musician at the turn of the twentieth century: how will society organize music making under socialism? Further, what would it mean to socialize music making under modern technological and productive conditions? In the decade before Adler's death, the composer Hanns Eisler gave a series of lectures on the historical materialist approach to music history to a classroom of KPD worker members. The text of those lectures has not yet been recovered. All the same, their existence indicates that a path of research lay open which, had historical contingencies not intervened, could have been followed.

Forces and Relations of Musical Production

In the world of art, as in the world of creation,
freedom and progress are the main objectives.

L. V. BEETHOVEN

• • •

Savages cannot build pianos;
this prevents them from playing the instrument or
composing pieces for it.

NIKOLAI BUKHARIN

• •
•

The preceding chapters reconstruct the project of classical musicology, high-lighting its orienting concern with the conditions of musical rightness (form-alism), as well as the patterns of stability and change in music's grammatical framework over time (style history). The aim has been to make perspicuous how a materialist conception of music history can directly inform this project by lending it a theory about the motive forces at work in historical processes. Bringing Marxism and musicology into discursive synthesis consists in wager-ing that musical rightness flows from the labour process. This is to say that the licenses and obligations to which musicians are compelled to adhere are proper to given relations of musical production, and further, that these rela-tions correspond to the normal degree of efficiency offered by a society's forces of musical production at any given place and time. To the extent that these very general notions can serve as skeleton for a body of concrete music historical phenomena, music history can be said to be amenable to historical material-ism.

That said, the task of fitting music historical concepts to a materialist frame-work is complicated by the fact that only the most elemental categories have been sufficiently clarified as to make the fit plausible. In his 1978 exposition of Marx's theory of history, G.A. Cohen described historical materialism as an 'infant science'. More recently, some have picked up on terminology introduced by the philosopher Imre Lakatos in characterising historical materialism as a 'degenerate research program'. The phrase connotes no moral risk, but rather expresses the fact that the set of theories about history the program encompasses has failed either to grow in an orderly fashion, or to bring into view significant novel facts about the dynamics of social change. Subsequent to Karl Kautsky's monumental *Materialist Conception of History* (1927) there was relatively little careful expository work on the subject until Analytic Marxists, well-tutored in clarity by the linguistic turn in philosophy, began publishing analyses of the most elementary categories of the method, including and especially, productive forces, relations of production, and social class. Since these are the best defined, it is useful to focus these as they relate to the specificity of musical production.

1   Forces and Relations

Strictly speaking, a productive force is not an object. Instead, an object *'has* productive power, the power to make or to be made into products'.[1] The set of objects with this capacity, then, naturally includes musical instruments of all kinds, the technologies of recording and amplification, concert halls and studios. Further, the set must also include less-tangible phenomena, such as systems of solmisation, notation and tuning. While a human being's capacity for creative labour is certainly a force of production, an individual need not be considered a force. In fact, this is a key distinction between capitalist and slave modes of production. The capitalist exploits the labour power of the worker by alienating it from individuals through exchange. The slave owner exploits his property directly, that is, as a force of production.

Relations of production are determined by the degree of control individuals have over the productive forces. They are statuses individuals can occupy with respect to anything in which productive power inheres, including objects and persons. Those statuses are selected for on the basis of their fitness to the technical means of production in any given sphere. While these means can be put to use by individuals who find themselves involved in a variety of social relations, we should expect that, all things being equal, those relations will tend to promote the efficient use of the available means. That said, nothing guarantees that the forces of production in every sector should develop at a similar rate, or in anything like the same manner. Textile production in England under-

---

1   Cohen 1978, p. 37.

went significant changes in the eighteenth century, resulting in a remarkable fall in the cost of cotton products by 1815.[2] No similar development occurred, for example, in the grinding of lenses. Lenses were ground on a modified potter's wheel and spun by means of a hand crank well into the nineteenth century. Only with mechanisation and steam power did production move out of the craftsman's workshop. Similarly, music making, by virtue of the special material conditions of its production, underwent technical advance unevenly and slowly relative to other sectors of the economy.

Within the music making system, as in any other sector of production, one expects to find stratification of various kinds. These are class stratifications when they involve ownership of the means of production in that sector. Importantly, individuals can be involved in the production process in more than one sector. The organist employed to enhance church services on Sunday mornings may also work a desk job during the week, and perhaps even collect rent from a tenant living in a room above his garage at the start of every month. The same person, then, can be an independent seller of high-skill services, an exploited employee, and an idle rentier in the space of a week. Social class, then, is only a category that becomes meaningful at a certain degree of elevation. Music history, in fact, is filled with characters who occupy more than once class position.

The aim in what follows is to illustrate the substance, and elucidate the promise, of a materialist approach to music history by discussing a purposefully wide range of music historical particulars in the terms just described. The scope is large, but not in the least exhaustive. Each topic addresses the determination of the relations of production among musicians by the forces of musical production. Special attention will also be paid to how the former shapes the musician's evolving class status. In each instance, it will be shown that technical innovations in the music making process can be said to drive its history forward.

2   Primitive Musical Communism

Gary Tomlinson's pathbreaking work on the gradual emergence of the human music making faculty over the course of the species' evolutionary history is a relevant place to start insofar as it understands music making in terms of technical achievements. His term is 'hominin technosociality'. Tomlinson self-

---

2 Scholars agree about the precipitous fall in prices, but not on the extent or cause. C.K. Harley and N.F.R. Crafts, 1995.

consciously abstracts from the division of musical labour, insisting that (nearly) all human beings are musicians in the sense that they display the fundamental capacities involved in both making music and appropriately responding to it. Indeed, his definition does not distinguish between playing and singing, on the one hand, and merely listening on the other. The capacities that allow for the former are equally involved in the latter, so that musicking is best understood as a collective possession of the species. The most elemental musically relevant capacity is entrainment, the ability to synchronize repeated actions. Entrainment not only allows for the 'technosocial' refinement of musical productive skill, but also for its transmissibility. In this way, a skill can form part of the general knowledge of a species, even before the emergence of language. 'In the history of stone toolmaking', for example:

> ... we can follow the sharpening mimetic capacities needed to trans-mit more and more intricate forms from one individual to another; this mimesis adumbrates entraining capacities akin to those that would underlie the more developed synchronies of musicking. We can follow also the offloading of technological transmission into mimetic culture – slowly at first, then more quickly – probably in part under the influence of the internal tendencies of the technologies themselves. In the wake of this offloading, technological variety finally burgeoned, as we would expect.[3]

Notably, Tomlinson conceives of culture, at least in its most primitive stages, as nothing more than the off-loading of skills to a shared transmission and propagation system. New capacity created by efficiencies such a system affords set the stage for the growth of new skills, as well as new needs met through them. Musical practices, in fact, display the enormous diversity that they do by virtue of this shared technosocial inheritance.

Given that the music making capacity is a common possession, we can at least conceive of a primitive musical communism, to wit, a means at the disposal of all which is employed in the flourishing of each. Further development of this capacity – 'the internal tendencies of the technologies themselves', no doubt – demanded that the refinement and transmission of musical skills be the power and responsibility of only some. It is intuitive that mastery of a specific musical skillset, for example, facility in playing one or more musical instruments, was best achieved through specialisation. We can therefore safely assume that the musical division of labour has an exceedingly long history.

---

3 Tomlinson 2013, p. 663.

3　　Minstrel and Chapel Singer

Around the turn of the eleventh century, the Russian *skomorokhi* underwent a 'process of transformation from local tribal cult leader to professional entertainer'.[4] These minstrel-entertainers persisted in Russian society for centuries, mastering any number of special skills, from musical performance to bear taming. By the middle of the sixteenth century, the city of Kazan had as many as eight working entertainment professionals. The *skomorokhi* exemplify the medieval division of labour, which joined the musical to any number of other capacities. The musical talents of neither the French *jongleur* nor the German *Spielmann* were cultivated exclusively. An independent minstrel could be hired to play instruments at table or in civic processions, perform tricks, or compose verse. The further refinement of specifically musical skills entailed a more granular division of labour. One Irish source from the early fourteenth century, for example, speaks of the death of 'Cam O'Kayrwill, that famous *tiompán* player and harper', who 'died along with twenty other *tiompán* players who were his students'.[5] The existence of a performance 'school' indicates that these players possessed a highly-developed, specialized performance skillset. However, whatever the degree of musical specialisation, the minstrel in early modern Europe enjoyed direct effective control over their means of production once these had been acquired. The services of a minstrel represented a form of social wealth, and like any other such form, it was disproportionately appropriated by a powerful minority. All the same, the minstrel's musicianship formed part of his very body. His personal possession of other means – an instrument, for instance – can be interpreted as a function of the corporeality of what it takes to make use of them. Absent the musician's person, harp, viol and shawm fall silent.

Singers stand out for not having recourse to any musical means apart from the body. Of course, this hardly entails any lack of sophistication in their music making. Anna Maria Busse Berger has detailed the extent to which singers relied on impressive practices of memory and recall, the sort which are proper to a largely illiterate society.[6] For centuries, singers who performed liturgical music learned a great many hours of monophonic song by heart. In order to accomplish this, there proliferated a variety of mnemonic devises, especially categorisation systems. These not only include devises such as the Guidonian hand, which afforded the student singer an intuitive and easily referenced

---

4　Zguta 1972, p. 299.
5　Buckley 2000, p. 175.
6　Busse Berger 2005.

map of pitch space, but also systems of modal classification, as well as much notated music. Practices of memorisation and recall are powerful means of musical production, and these were deliberately augmented and expanded as the art developed. By virtue of having built up 'memory cathedrals', to borrow a phrase, singers more easily acquired improvisational skills that allowed them to extemporize elaborations to the liturgy. A talented soloist at Notre Dame Cathedral in the late twelfth century could be expected to improvise organum using a set of internalized rules and without the aid of any written music. Even when written sources were available to singers, memory and improvisation remained indispensable musical means. The practice of 'singing upon the book', for instance, was widespread in Europe. This involved 'one singer [realising] the cantus firmus [...] while one or more other singers, called concentors, reading that same text, improvised a countermelody or melodies that responded to the cantus firmus while obeying the rules of counterpoint'.[7] It is clear that musical means that lived in the mind, and were therefore the stuff of personal property, were only very gradually off-loaded onto the page, and then only incompletely. Jessie Ann Owens and, more recently, Peter Schubert, have done much to reconstruct just how much of the music making faculty lived in the mind through at least the end of the seventeenth century.[8]

While both the minstrel and the trained singer in this period held in their person an impressive set of productive skills, it is in the nature of sung polyphony that the individual relinquishes full control over the endeavour. A singer has direct control over only a single part. The rules of counterpoint are designed to coordinate musical moves in an activity that is, in principle, collaborative. The product of trumpeters playing in unison is augmented in volume, timbre, and brilliance as the number of musicians increases. The matter is altogether different when voices sing in counterpoint. In a meaningful (even if not straightforwardly quantifiable) sense, more music is made by musicians 'singing upon the book' than by the same number performing a monophonic chant. This phenomenon is hardly unique to music. In the first volume of *Capital*, Marx notes that 'not only do we have here an increase in the productive power of the individual, by means of co-operation, but the creation of a new productive power, which is intrinsically a collective one'.[9] The monophonic song and improvised ensemble music that constituted the minstrel repertoire, then, underwent what Marx calls 'moral depreciation' in the face of polyphony. At the time of the death of Henry VII in 1509, the king counted

---

7   Broude 2020, p. 78.
8   Owens 1997; Schubert 2020.
9   Marx 1976 [1867], p. 443.

only minstrels and instrumentalists among his musical servants. By 1547, The King's Musick comprised fifteen singers and as many instrumentalists whose instruments lend themselves to the performance of polyphony. Churches and households that were able tended to afford themselves polyphonic music, and as a result, the demand for a minstrel's services declined. Even more damaging to the profession was artistic specialisation in fields outside of music. 'Once acting became a specialty separate from general minstrelsy', writes medievalist Timothy McGee, 'one of the most important and basic functions of the minstrel had been replaced by specialists. This reduced his services to mostly musical, and on that plane he competed unfavourably with the far more versatile – and fashionable – performers of polyphonic music'.[10]

Understanding elements of musical style in terms of productive capacity can help explain why they were broadly taken up. After all, growth in the forces of musical production is its own reward. However, this does not entail that all musical innovations are introduced with an eye to productive efficiency. Late medieval musicians innovated without the discipline of market competition that drives capitalist producers to constantly revolutionize the process of production. What is more, greater capacity is not always the sole or decisive factor determining when and where style change occurs. Advanced music making came up for criticism repeatedly, primarily from clerics and church reformers who saw in it a threat to piety. Beginning in the 1470s, for example, reformist sermonizers took aim at the achievements of fifteenth century polyphony in the context of their propagandising against corruption in the Church. A Dominican friar in Florence wrote in 1479 that 'certainly it would be much better that, following in the footsteps of the Holy Fathers, they should stick devoutly to that firm [...] and hence dignified and enduring chant, lest our mind should wander through pride and levity'.[11] Ideological commitment could forestall progress in music. That said, this motive force can be distinguished from the material compulsions of expanded technical capacity. The fate of early modern counterpoint is a case in point. Viewed from a sufficiently high elevation, we can note along with Reinhard Strohm that the whole of the fifteenth century 'is an enormous process of absorbing into art, or replacing by art, the shared archaic heritages'.[12] As polyphonic technique was enriched by the systematic integration of new intervals into the set of consonances, and the ability to represent precise note values to the eye, there arose in the fifteenth century a style of

---

10   McGee 1995, p. 103.
11   Quoted in Wegman 2005, p. 27.
12   Strohm 1993, p. 341.

mensural vocal polyphony that commanded authority throughout the continent, and constituted the grammatical basis for music making in Europe for
nearly two centuries. It should be noted that this process was itself dependent
on forces of production that were not stylistic in character. These include the
system of singing schools and the growth in chapel ensembles. The existence
of enough regularly constituted collaborative musical bodies was certainly a
necessary condition for the rise of Renaissance polyphony. That condition,
however, increasingly became a result as polyphony spread. Beginning as early
as the late fourteenth century, churches began combining endowments for services so as to hire singers. 'The supplication registers in the Vatican Archives
indicate unequivocally that requests for [combined endowments] were made
by the church and not by the pope', so we can be sure that the growth of new
ensembles resulted from new demand.[13]

If the chapel singer represented an advance on the minstrel in terms of the
process of production, it did not follow that the relations of musical production became any more free. Henry Raynor points out that 'during the fifteenth
and sixteenth centuries, boys whose beauty of voice was in any way matched
by their skill in reading music were not uncommonly whisked from one end of
Europe to the other, more frequently, of course from the musically developed,
urban north to Italy'.[14] He notes that the young Orlando di Lasso is reported
to have been abducted three times by nobles aiming to make use of the boy's
skills as a treble. If, following Maurice Dobb, we define relations of production
in terms of 'the relation between direct producer (whether he be artisan in
some workshop or peasant cultivator on the land) and his immediate superior
or overlord and in the social-economic content of the obligation with connects
them', and identify feudal relations with 'an obligation laid on the producer by
force and independently of his own volition to fulfilment certain economic
demands of an overlord',[15] then we can conclude that feudal relations were
long-lived in the music making system.

While some musicians were coerced into song by means of feudal obligation,
others could achieve a great deal of independent control over the developing
means of production. Indeed, the fifteenth and sixteenth centuries saw the
rise of the professional composer. Rob Wegman contends that the technical
conditions of, in particular, extemporized polyphony, lend themselves to differentiated responsibilities in the singing ensemble. One of the singers comes
to exert authority over the others in order to ensure musical success. He writes

---

13   Haggh 1989, p. 361.
14   Raynor 1978, p. 52.
15   Dobb 1946, p. 35.

that 'accumulated weight [of evidence] would seem to favour the hypothesis
that tenorists played a central, coordinating role in extemporized polyphonic
singing, and that it was they who would have been responsible for assuring
counterpoint approaching *res facta* in richness and control'.[16] The degree of
control that a composer could exert grew exponentially with the establishment of mensural polyphony, which requires the mediation of notation. The
case of Orlando di Lasso is unusual, but instructive. Beginning his career as an
impressed child singer, he ended it as the most widely published musician in
Europe. Lasso was the first composer to secure a royal privilege to control the
publication of his own works, first from the French king in 1571, and later from
the Holy Roman Emperor.[17]

Singers who did not become professional composers or secure lucrative
posts were frequently financially insecure and largely unable to determine their
own working conditions. Jonathan Glixon has detailed the efforts of members
of the *cappella* of San Marco in Venice to form a species of trade organisation
in the early 1550s. Competition among religious institutions for trained singers had caused there to be infelicitous rivalry among the city's most illustrious
musicians. These responded by organising what they termed a 'company', a
formal organisation that would effectively transfer a degree of control over the
allocation of, and compensation for, musical labour to musicians themselves.
Their charter states that:

> ... the singers named herein, [...] for the preservation of the peace and
> the increase in their earnings, in order to perform amicably all the feasts
> that are assigned to them, and to put together all of the earnings accru-
> ing therefrom to be divided among all in equal portions, as among good
> brothers, and in order to avoid all the disagreements that could easily
> arise and cause dissension and discord among them, and establish one
> all-inclusive Company, which will last as long as the lives of the mem-
> bers.[18]

The organisation would not be allowed to survive for long, as it came under
attack by the religious institutions in Venice that hired musicians. The impetus
to found trade organisations for musicians, however, persisted and in important ways, resembled that of other early trade union efforts. French journeymen
printers struck against their masters twice in the sixteenth century, once in

---

16   Wegman 1996, p. 445.
17   Wagner Oettinger 2004.
18   Glixon 1983, p. 399.

1539 and again in 1570. Often literate, printers were relatively well-prepared for self-organisation. In addition, 'printing demanded disciplined co-operation: three to four men worked a press together, and pressmen, compositors, and correctors tried not to keep each other waiting. As the journeymen said themselves, "we can't be compared to other artisans who work independently as they choose".[19] Chapel singers were similarly drawn together by the process of music making itself, compelled to operate in tightly regulated co-operation. This material condition of employment, then, had consequences in terms of the social relations most conducive to maximising the capacities of the relevant musical forces.

4   Thoroughbass and the Opera Industry

The efficiencies afforded by the thoroughbass are numerous and, by and large, in plain sight. Lodovico Viadana, the first composer to refer to a continuous bass (*basso continuo*) as a compositional element in a published composition, writes that the chief benefit of making use of such a bass line is that it allows the texture above it to vary considerably according to the available forces.[20] In vocal polyphony, the parts are constructed to fit together as a whole. Should a signer be unable to perform their part, the missing voice would result in incomplete sonorities and awkward pauses. 'The only way to patch up the performance', F.T. Arnold explains, 'was for the organist to fill the vocal gaps as best he could'.[21] A continuous bass line, independent of any given part and determining by way of melodic contour and annotations the rhythmic and chordal skeleton of an entire composition, not only secured performances against gaps in the texture, but also served to streamline the process of performing, improvising, composing, and teaching music. Thoroughbasses are remarkably flexible. In the first place, they allow for variability in terms of instrumentation, as basses can be realized by harpsichord or lute, bowed instrument or organ. Further, an accompanying musician can exploit that feature important to Viadana, and make judicious use of texture. The relative thickness of a realisation could be made appropriate to the nature and number of the accompanied voices. The same property allows a continuo ensemble to vary considerably in size without damaging the self-identity and structural soundness of a piece. Transposition is also made considerably easier.

---

19   Zemon Davis 1966, pp. 51–2.
20   Strunk 1950, pp. 419–20.
21   Arnold 1965, p. 5.

Instrumental performance of polyphonic lines was common performance practice throughout the sixteenth century. Indeed, only the singers of the Sistine Chapel were sufficiently insistent on continuity of tradition to keep their performances to voices alone. Scholars also agree that chordal accompaniments antedate the appearance of published thoroughbasses by many decades. The gradual development of an informal practice of improvising accompaniments was, in fact, a necessary condition for the establishment of the thoroughbass. The technical revolution began in earnest as musicians came to view polyphonic music as *in principle* regulated by a general bass, whether or not one appeared on the page. Given the expanded productive force the new practice represented, musicians all over Europe shifted their conceptual apparatus in the seventeenth century. In England, for example, thoroughbasses crop up just over a decade after Viadana's watershed 1602 publication. There is even evidence that by the end of his career Palestrina was compelled to append a basso continuo parts to his compositions.

The realisation of polyphony at sight from only a single horizontal line is only possible if a network of chordal and voice-leading conventions is memorized and intuitively categorized in the mind. The achievement is not all that unlike the medieval and early modern practices of memorisation and recall scholars have reconstructed. The most important difference lies in the degree of efficiency the thoroughbass achieved. Contemporaries were conscious that the device greatly improved the productivity of musical labour. In the first pages of his influential treatise on continuo, Johann David Heinichen describes the thoroughbass as labour-saving. 'With such methods [of systematic instruction in basso continuo]', he writes:

> ... the characteristic axiom and difference is that it is like an arithmetician solving a very difficult problem losing time calculating with general methods of computation, having smeared up half a quire and a lot more paper, whereas a learned algebraist can accomplish this and more at the same time in the blink of an eye. In the end, both accomplish their goal, however one has a clear advantage, whereas the other loses time and requires more effort.[22]

Because basso continuo's efficiencies depend on the deployment of patterns and conventions, it can be understood as a species of automation. A wave of research scholarship focusing on Italian *partimenti* has revealed the extent to

---

22   Brilmayer and Mongoven 2012, p. 2.

which musicians trained in the Neapolitan conservatory tradition made use of a large number of conventional bass line realisations which served as building blocks in both improvisation and composition. Partimenti are, in themselves marvels of efficiency. They largely consist of a single line of figured bass and were primarily designed for pedagogical purposes. Although they are inconceivable outside the context of thoroughbass practice, partimenti differ significantly in serving as the basis for a stand-alone composition. A line of basso continuo, by contrast, is designed to accompany one or more other parts. From only a single line, the skilled musician could improvise whole fugues at the keyboard. Advanced thoroughbass practice, then, served to partially automate the writing of counterpoint.

The foregoing points to a key feature of the technical advancement in question: the concentration of forces that were previously suited to co-operative employment in the hands of the individual musician. It is no coincidence that many of the figures that appear most prominently in historiography of the early thoroughbass era are solo singers who accompany themselves on a plucked instrument, often the lute. In reducing the minimal structural elements of a polyphonic composition to a solo voice and basso continuo, there is no longer a need for the most advanced musician to rely on others in the process of production. Something of the medieval minstrel's autonomy, then, is potentially restored. One of the singer-composers who embraced this affordance was Jacopo Peri (1561–1633). Peri specialized in composition designed to maximize the expressive potential of music for solo voice and chordal accompaniment, a genre music historians call 'monody'. By being among the first to publish dramatic verse in the monodic style, he is also recognized as one of the 'inventors' of opera. It is a matter of good fortune that copious and detailed records of his personal finances have survived. They offer unusually rich detail about the economic position of an influential musician at the turn of the seventeenth century.

In his monograph history of Western music, Richard Taruskin characterizes Peri as 'technically an aristocratic dilettante'.[23] The designation could well have been drawn from the published score for Peri's opera, *Euridice*, in which the composer describes himself as 'a noble Florentine'. However, as Tim Carter and Richard Goldthwaite have shown, Peri's class status is not so easily defined.[24] It is true that he counted Florentine citizens among his ancestors, but many of these were artisans, not landowners living off the agricultural labour of ten-

---

23   Taruskin 2010, p. 807.
24   Carter and Goldthwaite 2013.

ants or serfs. Peri was trained, first as a chapel singer and then, when his voice had broken, as a church organist. This latter form of employment, undertaken in his teens, already paid what an apprentice in the textile industry earned. Peri's Florence was a centre of early capitalism, home not only to merchant capitalists and bankers, but also to large and profitable manufactories of woollen cloths and silks. He was trained from an early age in Florentine accounting skills and kept records in his own hand. These reveal that his employment at the grand-ducal court, won primarily by virtue of his talents, was so well compensated that he was able to transform some portion of his income into capital even before he was married. Multiple marriages carried significant dowries, and Peri eventually secured ownership in land outside the city, a mark of high social status in its own right and, what is more, located in a fashionable part of the Tuscan countryside. As his personal wealth grew and his voice aged, Peri became increasingly active as an investor, both in woollens and in speculation.

Peri's personal class position is not uniform across his economic life. He occupied multiple social relations of production at once. As a musician at court, he was under obligation to provide musical services upon request. For these, he was not directly compensated. Rather, he secured a regular stipend from the court that lasted until his death. He was also granted access to less direct, but often no less lucrative, forms of compensation for his music making. As court musician, his obligations were feudal in the sense described above. Peri was, for example, expected to ask for leave to travel, and 'musicians could be tokens in the exchange of courtly favours, with both honor and prestige resting on the outcome'.[25] As an investor in industry and a lender at interest, however, Peri was a petty capitalist. He was also a landowner and collected rents associated with that property holding. Peri's complicated class status and variable ownership over diverse means of production serves to highlight the difficulties in fitting a single individual into a class category. These categories, in fact, reveal themselves to be blunt tools in biography. They become useful when abstracted from the experience of individuals and used to track, as we have been, the correspondence of the material conditions of production in a given sector to the operative social relations of production. Peri's music making made use of advanced musical technique, but was largely conducted under the same structure of feudal obligation that regulated the private musical establishments of princes.

Thoroughbass practice and the monodic style, however, did form the technical basis for musical services to be transformed into capital. This occurred

---

25   Carter and Goldthwaite 2013, p. 216.

in the context of commercial opera, which first appeared in Venice in the late 1630s. Opera production stands out in the history of music for coordinating and unifying the labour of otherwise independent musicians, dramatic poets, painters, and designers of stage machines. It thereby signals music's entry into what Marx might have called the 'manufacturing period' of the entertainment industry. This 'period properly so called, which extends, roughly speaking, from the middle of the sixteenth century to the last third of the eighteenth' – incidentally, the whole of the thoroughbass era – is defined 'by the assembling together in one workshop, under the control of a single capitalist, of workers belonging to various independent handicrafts, through whose hands a given article must pass on its way to completion'.[26] The grand-ducal court at Florence was, to a degree, able to achieve this kind of unifying and coordinating function. Carter and Goldthwaite even mention that the production of celebratory entertainments in that city bore a striking resemblance to the putting-out system that had developed in the cloth industry. Capitalist social relations, though, proved more amenable to the mode of production. The capitalist under whose control operatic production would take place represented a new type of businessman, the impresario. The impresario's business model took little time in solidifying once commercial opera had been introduced.[27] The theatres in Venice were built and owned by members of the official aristocracy. These were rented out as fixed capital to a producer, or else in the form of boxes to particularly wealthy opera-goers. Owners, therefore, would be guaranteed payment regardless of the success or failure of the opera. The financial risk was taken by the impresario, who controlled operations, hired and fired artists and workmen, and secured the capital investment. An impresario was only very rarely a musician. The composer Francesco Cavalli briefly organized and led an opera production company himself, but this was an early and exceptional case. As Ellen Rosand puts it, 'composers, [...] no matter how intelligent and well educated – and whatever the higher claims of music as theory – were essentially artisans, practitioners of a trade, for hire. Theirs was a service profession'.[28] The productive capacity that the individual musician could possess by means of thoroughbass practice was able to further strengthen the power of the composer over the music making process as a whole. As a factor of capital, however, that degree of autonomy was significantly attenuated. The efficiencies in terms of speed and flexibility in composition for soloist and continuo ensemble were

---

26   Marx 1976 [1867], p. 455.

27   The most detailed analysis of this model can be found in Glixon and Glixon 2006.

28   Rosand 1991, p. 210.

exploited by investors who demanded that new works be composed quickly and subject to numerous last-minute adjustments.

Having sold the product of their labour to capital did not mean that opera musicians had thereby become proletarian. The greater part of the means of musical production still resided in the musician's person, and so musicians did not sell their labour-power on the market, but were instead paid for their services. Of course, not all musicians possessed the same musical means, and some found themselves in stronger negotiating positions than others when it came to deciding on appropriate compensation. Composers and, especially, singers are particularly empowered by the conditions of production relative to ensemble performers or members of the chorus. Singers in Venetian theatres often had a noble caretaker who would act as a kind of agent, and command substantial fees. Compensation for stars, *prima donne* and *castrati*, remained exceedingly high through the following century. To the extent that they were employed by capital, however, they remained workers. Marx writes that 'the commodity produced by manufacture', in this case, a performance:

> ... from being the individual product of an independent craftsman, becomes the social product of a union of craftsmen, each of whom performs one, and only one, of the constituent partial operations, [...] but whatever may have been its particular starting-point, its final form is always the same – a productive mechanism whose organs are human beings.[29]

The status of being the human elements in a productive mechanism finds physical expression in Venetian innovations in stage design. The most important of these innovators, Giacomo Torelli, turned to the building of stage machines after employment in the Venetian Arsenal, one of Europe's most advanced industrial projects. The Arsenal's engineers had invented one of the earliest assembly lines, and at the peak of its efficiency, the ship manufactory could construct a seaworthy galley in a single day. Applying his expertise to the opera stage:

> Torelli's special contribution was to achieve those effects with a mechanical efficiency that enhanced the marvelous. By creating a central mechanism that controlled all the moving parts, he could set the entire stage into simultaneous motion. [...] No longer merely a backdrop of set-

---

29   Marx 1976 [1867], p. 457.

ting, the scenery actively participated in the drama, changing with, and as part of, the action.[30]

As fixed capital, Torelli's stage machines do not yet confront 'living labor as a ruling power and as an active subsumption of the latter under itself'.[31] Nevertheless, taking the form of fixed capital will come to have serious consequences for the means of musical labour.

5   The Musician Entrepreneur

The same ability for the musician to sell services to a production firm also allowed them to offer services on the open market. The master craftsman, after all, need not labour as a factor of production if it is possible to strike out on one's own. In the eighteenth century, a fraction of society's musicians was able to secure an independent income from making music. By virtue of his association with the English opera stage, Handel was able to live as a gentleman musician. Mozart incurred the ire of his ecclesiastical employer when he refused to return to Salzburg in 1781, and resolved instead to remain in Vienna to labor independently. Georg Knepler writes that 'it was [Mozart's] firm conviction that, being a bourgeois musician, no prince was superior to him in light of his gifts and achievements'.[32] The eighteenth century appears to inaugurate the era of the 'bourgeois musician'. Josef Haydn serves to exemplify the phenomenon. After decades at Esterházy, the aging composer could live in Vienna on the just rewards (much of it English) for his exceptional talent. The young Anton Reicha moved to commercial Hamburg from relatively provincial Bonn and successfully lived on income derived from teaching, demonstrating that even an unknown musician at the start of his career could successfully escape to the city and 'make it' on his own.

It is enticing to see the independent musician as an emblem of modernity. Enlightened anti-clericalism and anti-aristocratic sentiment predispose the historian to stress the apparent progress that independence from the two traditional contexts for musical employment – church and court – represents. Marxists inherit these values as a matter of ideological genealogy. They, at least, instruct us to look out for the evils of courtly employment and emphasize the heroism of those who shook off their feudal obligations. The virtuoso horn

---

30   Rosand 1991, p. 106.
31   Marx 1973 [1867], p. 693.
32   Knepler 1994, p. 82.

player, Jan Václav Stich, fled his Bohemian prince through stealth, and faced the knocking out of his front teeth had he been caught. The disfigurement would have robbed him of his means of musical production.[33] It is well known that J.S. Bach was imprisoned for attempting to leave his court appointment in Weimar in 1717.

Seeking a framework for interpreting the changing economic station of the musician in the eighteenth century, some music historians have been led to speak of musical entrepreneurship. Introducing an edited volume devoted to the theme, William Weber points to the erosion of the border between the profession and the business of music, but denies that the musical entrepreneur engaged in 'capitalistic speculation, that is, the furthering of large-scale profit through manipulation of markets'.[34] Rather, 'what was critical to the status of such people is that they were independent, standing outside licensed or monopolistic privilege and successfully manipulating a market in a public place'.[35] For Weber, the relevant distinction is between manipulative, monopolistic, speculative capitalism – an economic form that comes in for scorn in his account – and the self-promoting, self-managing entrepreneur. This latter embodied 'petty capitalism in its most basic form, a world in which the main goal was not so much to maximize profit as to coordinate social circumstances in such a fashion as to maintain a satisfactory cash flow'.[36] In celebrating musical entrepreneurship, Weber is able to focus his readers on the hard realism of social history, as opposed to abstract discussions of compositions and their content. He also self-consciously breaks with what he calls 'Marxist historical perspectives', which, among other things assumes 'an objectively defined money system' which, Weber claims, recent scholarship has revealed to be an anachronism in the context of the eighteenth century.

Distinguishing Weber's political economic assumptions from Marxism is a relatively straightforward matter. First, the distinction between a parasitic, monopolistic, and speculative capitalism and another, simpler, fairer, and less profit-motivated kind, is not a meaningful one in *Capital*, where the difference between large and small capitals is one of size, not kind. Further, the musician who organizes his own concert tour, does his own playing, and then collects the proceeds is not engaged in capitalist profit seeking at all. At no point does this independent musician invest money capital in a valorisation circuit for the purposes of securing a return that might be reinvested in another cycle

---

33 Carlton 2006, p. 9.
34 Weber 2004, p. 6.
35 Weber 2004, p. 8.
36 Weber 2004, p. 108.

of production. Whatever Weber means by 'an objectively defined money system', the conception does not leave room for the distinction between price and value. Importantly, the concept of the musical entrepreneur is a historiographical, theoretical one. The word 'entrepreneur' existed in the eighteenth century, but it was not commonly used to refer to the status of musicians. While many musicians were able to make careers without a court or church position, it was never the case that this option represented a new phase in the social relations of musical production. Some musicians became independent, but all could not. Finally, 'entrepreneur' is not strictly an economic category. Instead, it refers to features of a personality: a willingness to take risks, an ability to discover new markets, an orientation to consumer demand.

The discourse of entrepreneurship is thoroughly contemporary, rather than historical. The attempt to uncover the history of musician entrepreneurs comes at a moment when musicians are being tasked with inventing the conditions for gainful self-employment, and therefore encouraged to think as an entrepreneur. A mounting literature on the subject is routinely marketed to those who have recently graduated from music schools and find little economic opportunity in the open market for the use of their hard-won skills. In *The Entrepreneurial Muse*, Jeffrey Nytch writes that 'while entrepreneurship may not reveal a uniform replacement for the traditional [model of support for arts institutions], it absolutely *can* help the individual performer or organisation develop the best business model for their particular venture'.[37] Nytch does not see a viable future for large production companies with high fixed costs, as they operate on low margins despite offering a luxury product. 'In contrast', he notes, hopefully, 'it's a lot easier to find success stories – and hope for the future of classical music – when looking at chamber groups and individuals rather than the entrenched, low-margin, behemoth symphony orchestra'.[38] Responding to negative employment trends, music schools have also taken on the discourse of musical entrepreneurship, offering courses and workshops on the subject. The topic is most often presented as a dose of economic realism in the context of an otherwise rarified artistic education. That realism, however, is tempered by the fact that no amount of entrepreneurialism can make up for the shortfall in employment opportunities for professionally trained musicians. Some will succeed, and most will fail. Neither a historical designation, nor properly considered a political economic category, the musical entrepreneur is best understood as an ideological concept. Its usefulness lies in the ethics about the

---

37   Nytch 2018.
38   Nytch 2018, p. 160.

marketplace it entails. When attempting to understand the class position of the musician in the eighteenth century, we do well to avoid colluding with contemporary ideology, even if that era's celebrated liberalism seems to invite it.

6   Organised Musical Labor

If the age of the 'bourgeois musician' never materialized, one of the reasons has to do with a more granular division of musical labour that had fully taken hold by the start of the nineteenth century. The thoroughbass musician was displaced by the performance specialist. Paul Henry Lang has it that:

> ... after the middle of the [eighteenth] century the music came to [the musician] in a finished form, and if he mastered his instrument to a degree he could play almost anything; his only problems were technical. [...] As the old art of improvisation, continuo playing, and 'mental counterpoint' disappeared, little was left to the imagination; the scores carried ample instructions for every detail. The professional musician soon felt the repercussions of this trend. As their technical ability increased, their formerly universal musical training and knowledge decreased.[39]

The ability for the individual musician to possess all the means of the most advanced musical production eroded as the multi-instrumentalism that had been common in previous centuries gave way to specialisation, particularly in those instruments that formed part of standard ensembles. The orchestra, which expanded over the course of the ninetieth century in terms of size, volume and timbral variety, was able to perform ever larger and more difficult works as this trend progressed. The expanded productive capacity this entailed served to reinforced the process. In his 1926 textbook on historical materialism, Nikolai Bukharin observes that:

> ... the distribution of the members of an orchestra is determined precisely as in the factory, by the instruments and groups of instruments; in other words, the arrangement and organisation of these members is here conditioned by musical technique [...] and, through it, based on the stage in social evolution, on the technique of material production as such.[40]

---

39   Lang 1941, p. 725.
40   Bukharin 1925.

The effective control that any given orchestral musician is able to exert over the whole of the music making process diminished as ensembles grew in size and sophistication.

The material conditions of production, then, were such that it made good sense for musicians to organize collectively. Musicians themselves, however, were exceedingly slow in coming to this conclusion. In the United States, musicians had begun to self-organize in the Civil War period – which is to say, in the first decades of the labour movement – but these had only very local reach and conceived of themselves primarily as fraternal organisations. As such, they did not differ significantly from the International Order of Odd Fellows.[41] These local clubs regulated the musical wage scale, but merely as an extension of their mission to provide mutual assistance to fellow professionals. As travel became cheaper and competition among musicians fiercer, the need for a nation-wide organisation for the protection of musicians' interests was met by the founding of the National League of Musicians in 1886. The League enforced its wage standards by doing what it could to prevent union musicians from playing with non-members, and it took up the cause of protecting the jobs of native-born musicians over foreign-born. None of these functions, so characteristic of a trade union, had the effect of convincing organisational leadership to directly associate itself with the broader labour movement. Musical unionism predates class consciousness among musicians by decades.

This is partly reflective of the fact that, while technological advancements had been introduced into the production process – piston valves became standard in horns, for example, and many instruments were designed to make a louder sound – none had automated it. Unlike skilled craft professionals across the economy, musicians were not faced with replacement by machines. Instead, employment opportunities grew for musicians as cities became more populous and the entertainment and leisure industries boomed. The fraction of the labour force that was engaged in making music grew quickly as the twentieth century approached. These workers were not routinely joined together in large productive facilities, but mainly secured gig work from 'leaders' who would use the union to scout for talent, or 'sidemen'. A leader, for their part, would be paid for organising musical services by a capitalist, often a venue owner. Individual musicians, then, even if they exclusively played in combination with others, and even while their services were factors of capitalist production, retained a relatively high degree of autonomy over their working lives.

---

41   For an account of fraternal organizations as class organizations, see Clawson 1985.

Inevitably, however, the League's steady refusal to acknowledge the objective class status of musicians led to the organisation's demise. The American
Federation of Labor repeatedly approached the League about affiliation, but
organisational leadership balked. Newer branches, which were mostly concen-
trated in the West and the Midwest, favoured coordinating with the broader
labour movement. Larger and older branches on the east coast, however, 'still
bemused by the artist-labourer dichotomy, shunned any association with a
trade-union'.[42] The internal division split the organisation in 1896, with the
much greater share of membership choosing to affiliate with the AFL as part of
a new union, the American Federation of Musicians. The League was disban-
ded less than a decade later, and when the AFM incorporated those members,
it came to represent the vast majority of the nation's professional musicians.
By all measures, the AFM represented a powerful and successful craft union.
Its membership would continue to grow in absolute numbers until 1976, and it
remains in existence.[43] So it is that when automation did, finally, threaten to
replace the musical worker, its implementation had to contend with organized
labour.

The second decade of the last century saw the maturity of a series of technologies that allowed a live musician to be replaced by a loud speaker. The
historian James Kraft writes that:

> ... the development of new sound technologies into the mainstream of
> commercial activity transformed the musicians' world, turning a diffused,
> labor-intensive, artisanal structure into a centralized, capital-intensive,
> highly mechanized one.[44]

Sound recording augments the reach of an individual performance and serves
to preserve it. Its labour-saving potential is, there, substantial, if not breathtak-
ing. To the extent that fidelity and relative quality of performance can make a
recording just as – or more – valuable than a live event, musicians will be displaced. Radio technology, too, puts a musician's services in direct competition
with, to coin a phrase, mechanical reproduction. However, arguably the most
disruptive technology to musical employment was synchronized sound in film.

Competition between capitals does tend to produce innovation and maximize efficiencies, but not of all kinds. Musicians, in particular, are familiar

---

42   Countryman 1948, p. 58.
43   The statistics are helpfully compiled in Moore 1991.
44   Kraft 1996.

with tools and techniques that are not the product of industrial production, or even competition between commodity producers. The form of musical mechanisation embodied in the pipe organ, for example, is not responsive to the felt need to maximize profit and control over the workplace. Its primary usefulness is not to save on wages as a portion of capital invested. Synchronized sound in film, however, was adopted precisely for the purposes of replacing live musicians in movie theatres. In the silent era, live accompaniment was expected, and elite movie palaces representing large capitals competed with smaller theatres in part by accompanying films with large bands, and in some cases, full orchestras. These latter routinely featured wilful conductors who exercised their power over the music making by routinely ignoring scoring cues published by the film studios. Film accompaniment ensembles, whatever their size, adopted the same owner-leader-sidemen model that had been operative since before the turn of the century. It was, therefore, a form of employment amenable to the union. The pits of movie theatres were closed shops, and music's part in the entertainment was so important that a strike among its musicians would cripple a theatre. Films, sometimes preceded by short musical entertainments or else punctuated by live acts, many of which also featured music, were so successful a segment of the entertainment industry that movie theatres came to employ roughly a third of unionized musical labour by the time synchronized sound became available. The Vitaphone, and then the integrated soundtrack, allowed theatre owners to dispense with demanding and organized workers. When:

> ... in April 1926, [...] Western Electric (Bell's production arm) and Warner Brothers Pictures jointly announced an agreement concerning the Vitaphone, they made it clear that the sole immediate goal in the movie industry was to replace live music in movie theaters with mechanical recordings. This announcement did not reveal any intentions of recording movie dialogue in the future.[45]

The move increased profits by throwing off labour, and extended the control of the capitalist over the production process. The tastes of movie goers quickly adapted.

Synchronized sound brought about mass unemployment among professional musicians, and while the AFM campaigned to protect employment in the sector, its efforts were plainly never going to be enough to permanently

---

45   Hubbard 1985, p. 430.

stave off the implementation of a profit-maximising technology. The largest capitals in entertainment, to whatever extent they could, employed musicians by placing them in front of a microphone. When he was elected President of the AFM in 1958, Herman Kenin declared that 'canned music' remained 'the all-pervasive challenge to our profession and to our union'.[46] The statement is striking given that it was made over a decade after his predecessor, James Petrillo, had enforced a highly publicized recoding ban from 1942 to 1944. That action, directed at balancing the interests of musical labour with those of entertainment capital, stood little chance of success. In the midst of the ban, Petrillo appeared at a Senate committee hearing in part to defend the contractual stipulation that union members be hired at radio stations to change sides on records, a job known as 'platter turning'.[47] This detail stands out, if for no other reason than because it puts one in mind of Karl Marx in the so-called 'Fragment on the Machine' from the *Grundrisse*. In the dead labour of the record and the machinery that plays it, 'knowledge appears as alien, external to [the worker]; and living labour [as] subsumed under self-activating objectified labour. The worker appears as superfluous to the extent that his action is not determined by [capital's] requirements'.[48] With the removal of the vast majority of capital's requirements for living musical labour, trade unionism declined precipitously in the American music industry.

7   After Capitalism

Noting that the advent of sound film 'gives good reasons to anticipate the complete mechanisation of music of these places of entertainment in the next decade', the English music critic Henry Raynor wrote that:

> Fascism in Britain would confer on the musical profession the right to elect its own representatives to voice its demands in the legislative assembly. Purely musical questions it would settle of its own accord, to the satisfaction of the interests of the profession. Thus, the question of the State control of music does not arise, but the State makes the path along which music will progress.[49]

---

46   The quotation appears in Seltzer 1989, p. 74.
47   Peterson 2013.
48   Marx 1973 [1857–8], p. 695.
49   Raynor and Stevens 1934, pp. 737–38.

Raynor's 1934 endorsement of the British Union of Fascists' plan to respond to the ruination of the musical worker by automation is notable for the role it holds out for 'the musical profession'. This is a euphemism for an institution which presumably corresponds to a musician's union without, of course, being identical to the Musicians' Union of the United Kingdom. This image of musical corporatism amounts to tacit acknowledgment that, should the whims of capital investment be allowed to determine the nature and extent to which music is made, the art itself might suffer, and society become poorer as a result.

While both the UK's Musicians' Union and the AFM were successful labour organisations for a time, neither endorsed socialism. Militancy and political ambitions have only declined with membership. In 2015, the MU endorsed Andy Burnham over Jeremy Corbyn for Labour leader in a move that expressed its enduring conservatism.[50] The end of a period that saw most working musicians in trade unions has meant that it is ever less intuitive for musicians to identify with explicitly working-class politics. Certain that so long as it cuts down on cost, capital will divest from living musical labour, socialists have reason to appeal to this part of the workforce. We should also be mindful that our own vision of a post-capitalist future for music making will eventually compete with those from the far Right.

Given the presupposition that relations of production tend to be fit to the prevailing forces of production in a given sector, the question of a musical socialism – or even, a musical communism – hinges on the tools society has at its disposal for meeting its musical needs. Given technology already available, it is conceivable that most in a socialist society could become musically literate. In a productive system geared to expanding its forces of production by increasing the number of competent musicians, we could expect general musical skills to reach a high enough level that most are able to participate in music making, both on a small scale for domestic use, and as part of large-scale ensembles when greater forces are called for. Music making as such could come under democratic control at the level of society as a whole, and any anarchy in its production could be overcome through a common plan. The establishment of any form of musical socialism, however, cannot come about by accident. It is a feature of this mode of production that it must be carried on self-consciously.

We do well, then, to consider musicology itself as a productive force, the development of which has the capacity to inform changes in the relations of musical production. Indeed, Cohen takes it that 'the development of know-

---

50   Williamson and Cloonan 2016.

ledge is [...] the center of the development of the productive forces'.[51] Allied to socialist construction, a materialist musicology in full flower could provide a rational basis for consciously adopting relations of production that maximize the potential of a musically wealthy society. Brought under the control, not only of its immediate producers, but of all toilers, the music making system could escape its prehistory and further develop along lines set out for it by those whose needs it meets.

---

51   Cohen 1978, p. 45.

The Harmonic Ideology

> The chief defect of all hitherto existing materialism [...] is that the thing, reality, sensuousness, is conceived only in the form of the object or of contemplation, *but not as* sensuous human activity, practice.
>
> KARL MARX, 'Theses on Feuerbach'[1]

∴

This book argues for the relevance, appropriateness, and usefulness of historical materialism to the musicological project. Its scope is determined by the contemporary borders of the discipline, and therefore leaves out of account historical musicology's sister disciplines, namely, music theory and ethnomusicology. Taking up a similar project with the latter deserves a separate study, given the long history of Marxist engagement with anthropological method and the necessity of surveying an expansive Soviet literature on the topic.[2] The Soviet Union's ethnic diversity combined with a political commitment to promote national self-determination in the cultural sphere to produce fertile conditions for vernacular music research. By contrast, music theory is less intuitively amenable to adopting a historical materialist method. In fact, the discipline's penchant for formal abstraction and minimal concern for history has tended to inspire suspicion among Marxists, both in the Soviet period and since. This is not to say that no music theoretical writing exists in the tradition.[3] One need only mention the legacy of Boris Asafiev.[4] Rather, the differences between historical and analytical methods suggest that the Marxist might approach the latter with scepticism, even critique.

---

1 Marx 1992, 421.
2 See Krader 1990.
3 See McQuere 1983.
4 The work of Boris Asafiev, for example, whose conception of "intonation" proved lastingly influential, deserves both more robust commentary, and for his works to be more easily accessible in English. For more on Asafiev, see Tull 1976.

1   Theory or Reference?

In the literature, of course, critique of this kind most often appears as the critique of ideology. The term is something of a Marxist cliché, a derogatory way to refer to mental conceptions promoted by ruling classes and designed to perpetuate their political dominance by obfuscating real social conditions. 'Ideology', writes the sociologist Christian Fuchs, 'is a strategy of reproducing domination and exploitation that operates in the realms of communication, culture, psychology, emotions, and beliefs'.[5] On this account, nothing in principle distinguishes ideological domination from other forms of political repression, including judicial punishment and police violence, except the means employed. These means are particularly insidious because they aim to overthrow agency. The victim of ideological corruption is liable to consent to their own exploitation and engage in political struggle that militates against their economic interests.

The critique of ideology is so prevalent today that it is difficult to imagine it ever having been otherwise. It is nevertheless the case that the contemporary concern with 'ideology' is of relatively recent vintage. Marx, for instance, makes no mention of it in any volume of *Capital*. Neither does it appear in Karl Kautsky's *The Class Struggle* (1892) or *The Road to Power* (1909). For her part, Rosa Luxemburg feels no need to take up the term in any of her major writings. Among those authors that make up what Perry Anderson calls 'the classical tradition', the word is, as often as not, a neutral term, most often used to refer to a set of philosophical or political commitments. So it is that Antonio Labriola can use it as a synonym for idealism in philosophy, and the Stalin-era 'Short Course' on the history of the Russian Communist Party can refer to both bourgeois and Bolshevik ideology without necessarily connoting deprecation or invoking critique.[6]

Contemporary usage stems from that branch of the literature Anderson calls 'Western Marxism', where the topic of philosophical and political commitments is subsumed under a theory of mind, or what Habermas referred to as a 'critique of knowledge'. In his *Knowledge and Human Interests* (1968), Habermas chides Marx – and, by extension, his successors in the parties of the Second and Third Internationals – for failing to extricate his conception of ideology from the 'categorial framework of production'.[7] On his view, an account escapes

---

5   Fuchs 2020, 217.
6   Labriola 1908; and Brandenberger, David and Mikhail Zelenov (eds.) 2019.
7   Habermas 1987.

this framework by analysing the material conditions of cognition as such. A philosophically sophisticated approach in this vein can only be said to have begun in earnest after the Second World War, and it owes at least as much to Georg Lukács and Antonio Gramsci as it does to Marx or Engels.[8] Its chief exponent in the period since the collapse of the Soviet state has been the cultural theorist Slavoj Žižek, for whom ideology is defined by what a subject is not conscious of knowing. 'The very concept of ideology', he writes, 'implies a kind of basic, constitutive *naïveté*: the misrecognition of its own presuppositions, of its own effective conditions, a distance, a divergence between so-called social reality and our distorted representation, our false consciousness of it'.[9] Importantly, this description decentres the known contents of philosophical and political commitments, in other words, precisely what the classical usage referred to.

The most conspicuous appearance of the word among the writings of the Founders is in the title of their unpublished early manuscript, *The German Ideology*. The apparent prominence of this usage, however, must be qualified by the fact that, borrowing a memorable phrase from Terrell Carver, '*The German Ideology* never took place'. As Carver is at great pains to show, both book and title are editorial artifacts.[10] The title does not appear at the head of the manuscript. Instead, it first appears in a note written in 1847 that refers to a manuscript on the topic of 'the German ideology'. There, it appears in quotation marks, a coined phrase. Indeed, in the middle 1840s it serves as a reference to what one could call 'the French ideology', namely the materialist 'science of ideas' associated in the first place with the liberal aristocratic intellectual Antoine Destutt de Tracy (1754–1836). Little known and rarely studied today, Tracy voraciously assimilated a vast literature on topics ranging from physics to political economy in an effort to discover the material foundations for phenomena which had proved resistant to materialist explanation. Importantly, these included historical and social phenomena. He introduced the term 'ideology' to describe the field he took himself to have founded, and did so primarily to distinguish it from both metaphysics and psychology, disciplines he felt were overgrown with archaic spiritualism. Intentionally leaving to one side the Romantic strain in philosophy from Rousseau through Kant, Tracy drew on Diderot and Helvétius in constructing a philosophy of everything, including grammar, logic, the will, marriage, and political economy. Marx himself cites the Frenchman's work on the last of these. Tracy's books, which began to appear just after the turn of the

---

8   Larraín 1979.
9   Žižek 1989, 24.
10   Carver 2010.

nineteenth century popularized his neologism and were enthusiastically read not only in Europe, but also in the Americas. Enlightened politicians, including Thomas Jefferson, intent on replacing the action-guiding content of faith with the cutting edge of modern reason could find in Tracy a basis for modern government. The strong association of this intellectual project with republicanism eventually led Napoleon Bonaparte to polemicise against it as he went about re-establishing of the trappings of feudal absolutism. It was the French emperor's derisive and ironic references to the new science of ideas that form the basis for the most common use of the word today. Tracy's hefty tomes on 'ideology', meant to outline a new science, were the first in history to be dismissed as mere ideology.

Marx picks up this Napoleonic irony when he refers to a '*German* ideology', by which he means a specific philosophical school, namely, the Young Hegelian movement to which both he and Engels belonged at the time of writing. Like the French *idéologues* Marx compares them to, these writers proposed to introduce a materialist system to serve as post-Christian legitimation for the activities of the citizens of a modern republic. Support for just such a republic, in fact, united French and German counterparts, and hence one can detect an echo in this reference to Marx's commentary on Goethe, published in the same period. In a book review for the *Deutsche Brusseler Zeitung*, he explains ambivalences in the poet's personality as expressing what he calls the 'German *misère*', that nation's relative economic backwardness with respect to England, and its political backwardness with respect to France. Feuerbach's secular Hegelian anthropology, coming as it does from a largely pre-industrial country with no republic to defend against authoritarian regression, plays less developed cousin to Destutt de Tracy's *idéologie*.

That a literary or historical refence should come to name a theoretical concept is nothing new in Marxism. The phrase 'industrial proletariat', for example, includes a reference to a census category in ancient Rome. In the case of ideology, and for our purposes here, however, we might retain the insights of the reference at the expense of a theory of knowledge, and proceed by analogy. A critique of music theoretical discourse can begin by analogising its original program to the republican materialism shared by both French and German ideologies. To the extent that this holds, it can serve as the basis for a socialist materialist successor program, as the critique of the German ideology did for Marx and Engels.

2   Theoretical Harmony

Music theory's modern theoretical program originates as a theory of harmony. A Copernican turn in the science of music is universally credited to the organist, composer, and *philosophe* Jean-Philippe Rameau (1683–1764), who set out to demonstrate that the simultaneously sounding melodies that ostensibly constitute a musical texture are, in reality, governed in their surface-level motion by harmonic motion. There exists, then, a distinction between a harmony and a chord. If two or more voices articulate their rhythmic alignment by arriving at pitches which, sounding together, form satisfactory consonances, we can justifiably refer to the whole simultaneity as a chord. Harmonies, on the other hand, are theoretical entities, and pre-exist any given instance of music making. A chord in four parts, made up of an octave, a third, and a fifth above a given bass pitch, represents the audible expression of what we can call 'perfect harmony'. Since these intervals exhaust the set of possible consonances that can be sounded together satisfactorily over a bass note, this four-part representation can be classed as a perfect realisation of perfect harmony. Chords made up of only two or three voices cannot exhaust the set of possibilities, and are therefore imperfect realisations of perfect harmony. Chords of five or more voices can offer no more than compound versions of the same intervals; thus, their representative status is uncontroversial.

Chords made up of an octave, a sixth, and a third are no less made up of consonances, but the presence of the sixth entails the absence of the fifth, which is the more consonant interval. Harmonic theory interprets these chords as inverted representations of perfect harmony. If one understands the sixth above the bass as an inverted third – the note G-sharp sounding above E rather than below it, for example – then this pitch can be identified as corresponding to the fundamental bass note, even though it is not the lowest sounding pitch. Similarly, a chord made up of an octave, a sixth and a fourth represents perfect harmony. The fourth sounds a dissonance above the bass that might be resolved down by step to form a third. Indeed, contrapuntal manuals listed the fourth among those dissonances in need of resolution. Through the lens of harmony, however, it becomes an inverted fifth, and, far from being excluded from the harmony, represents the harmonic fundamental.

The modern theory of harmony distinguishes itself from its predecessors precisely in providing an account of the special laws of musical motion. Whatever the status of the realisation, perfect harmonies do not drive changes in harmony, and cannot fully account for harmonic progression. Their stability, in fact, is essential to them. Another type of harmony must therefore be posited, one pregnant with motive force, like a compressed spring. This second species of harmony is made up of all the intervals of perfect harmony with an added seventh above the fundamental. This note lies a third above the fifth of the harmony, and apparently arrives as a consequence of a pattern of stacked thirds that characterizes the perfect triad. The dissonance inherent to this type of harmony demands resolution, and so generates both harmonic progression and its representation in voice-leading. Harmonies of the seventh, like perfect harmonies, can be expressed in inversion, and their power to determine musical motion can persist even if ostensibly constitutive features of the harmony (say, a seventh's fundamental note) is not sounded. Harmonic dissonance, then, differs considerably from contrapuntal dissonance insofar as this quality pervades harmonies as such, rather than characterising a specific relation between two voices.

As with ideologies French and German, modern harmonic theory is offered up as a materialist alternative to an intellectual inheritance beholden to mystical dogma. Premodern harmonic theory is decidedly ancient, and not restricted to the science of relating pitches. The Pythagorean school held that the simple arithmetical divisions of the monochord that result in consonances are instances of a more general harmony that binds the world together. For a Pythagorean at the turn of the third century before the common era, the theory of harmony described the manner in which an unlimited thing – like earth, water, or fire – could come to occupy a limited shape. These two dialectically opposed substances, the limited and the unlimited, are neither conflated nor sublated, but rather hang together in harmony. Indeed, the Greek word at issue originally referred to a joint of the kind one might use to build a ship. Picking up the same line in the seventeenth century, Athanasius Kircher reckoned the world, like a ship, 'bound by secret knots'. The premodern theory of harmony was suffused with references to music (Kircher's treatise includes whole compositions) but the wonders of plucked strings were ultimately incidental to its wider aim, namely, a metaphysical account of the orderliness of the universe. Rameau's successor program for the theory of harmony is self-consciously, even spectacularly, deflationary. Far from explaining anything universal, modern harmony seeks the source and governing laws of one and only one kind of motion: the apparently orderly way that musical voices tend to move.

To this end, Rameau takes up a mechanical view of musical motion, directly in line with the very Enlightened French materialism Destutt de Tracy sought to expand and update. Rameau writes that 'if we allow ourselves to speak of these sounds as if they were solids, we might say that they touch each other and collide with each other, for this is certainly similar to the effect they produce on the ear'.[11] Harmonic progression, then, is just a matter of tracking the spring-loaded billiard balls that organize musical motion from behind the scenes. The mechanical analogy is a powerful one, and has lost little of its usefulness and authority in the intervening centuries. A representative quotation makes the point:

> We *hear* music *as* purposeful activity within a dynamic field of musical forces. Those forces include 'gravity' (the tendency of an unstable note to descend), 'magnetism' (the tendency that grows stronger the closer we get to a goal), and 'inertia' (the tendency of a pattern of musical motion to continue in the *same* direction where what is meant by 'same' depends on what that musical pattern is 'heard as'). One might say that we experience melodic implications as if generated by these (and perhaps other) musical forces.[12]

These mechanics, of course, are not apparent, only posited. The analogy expresses the post-mystical conception of musical laws as natural laws.

One might feel that musical forces are at work in any given instance of voice-leading, but the harmonic plane to which they are native is notoriously difficult to access. To paraphrase Marx, polyphony's 'secular basis detaches itself from itself and establishes itself as an independent realm'.[13] It is a testament to the resiliency of harmonic materialism that competing accounts of how harmonies are generated can leave the rest of the theory's explanatory framework almost entirely intact. The source of that resiliency, however, is precisely the gap between the determined harmonic realm and its audible expression. This feature of the theory was demonstrated by Rameau himself, who substituted a physical for a geometrical theory of harmonic generation in light of advancements in the physics of sounding bodies. In the first edition of his *Treatise on Harmony* (1722), he relies on the oldest known method for arriving at perfect harmony, namely, by division of the monochord, a musical instrument cum scientific demonstration consisting of a single string. However, once he encountered the overtone series, he was quick to adopt it as the source of his theory's elemental units. It served Rameau's purposes well to argue that consonances were always already contained within the pitched sound of any resonant body. No operation, apart from plucking, need be performed on a string to demonstrate its harmonic properties. In resonating, a monochord divides

---

11   Rameau 1971, 78.
12   Larson 1994, 44.
13   Marx 1992, 422.

itself. A perfect triad, then, can be heard as an abbreviated summary of the series, a model of a reality just beyond direct perception. In second half of the nineteenth century, the material basis for harmonic generation shifted again. The study of human sensation had turned to physiology. The assumption that objects in the world make direct impression on our biologically endowed sensing apparatus was abandoned. The form and function of our sense organs – the cones and rods of the eyeball, and the differentiated role of each eyeball in binocular vision – could now be assumed to contribute constitutively to experience. In his *On the Sensations of Tone as a Physiological Basis for the Theory of Music* (1863), Hermann von Helmholtz sought to ground harmonic theory in what can be known about the acoustic perception of tones. Combination tones, for example, which encompass multiple frequencies that are resolved in the ear, contrast with the perception of interference between frequencies. Notably, Helmholtz moves closer to a thoroughgoing materialism by identifying a role for history. The affordances of acoustic perception set the stage for musical progress, which gradually discovered harmonic theory in the course of its technical development. Helmholtz concedes that aesthetic principles cannot be studied in a laboratory setting. In fact 'the only observations and experiments [...] to which we can appeal, are those which mankind themselves have undertaken in the development of music'.[14] He was, therefore, gratified to discover in a statistical analysis of a *Stabat Mater* by Palestrina that the Renaissance master, having no special knowledge about the human ear, had nonetheless preferred chordal voicings that maximize the perception of harmonic euphony.[15]

Harmonic theory's abstraction has long had its discontents. The esteemed English music critic Sir Donald Tovey writes that the fundamental bass –

> ... is an imaginary bass (best when imaginary) that gives 'roots' to all the essential chords of the music above it. The conception is true only of the most obvious harmonic facts; beyond them it is as vain as the attempt to ascertain your neighbor's dinner from a spectrograph of the smoke from his chimney.[16]

If Rameau's achievement was to reduce musical motion to that which was most concrete, the properties of sounding bodies, then it is not without irony that fundamental bass analysis can leave even a sensitive musician and accom-

---

14   Helmholtz 1954, 249.

15   Kursell 2015.

16   From Tovey's article on "Harmony" from the 14th Edition of the Encyclopedia Britannica. Quoted in Lloyd 1939.

plished composer with just so much chimney smoke. Jairo Moreno, in a Fou-cauldian vein, generates harmonies by means of the 'classical episteme', pur-posefully focusing on the self-consistency of discourse at the expense of rep-resentative success. Referring to a composition by Rameau himself, Moreno writes that 'to the eye or ear neither fundamental bass nor dissonances exist as the sound of the [piece]; they are instead echoes of the murmuring voices of analysis, cognitive interventions motivated by theoretical claims to know-ledge'.[17] Harmonic theory's longstanding success, in fact, hinges on its relatively high altitude, which leaves ample room for theoretical creativity, as well as license to leave major problems unsolved. To wit, by the turn of the twenti-eth century, Hugo Riemann had extended harmonic theory to include a theory of harmonic functions, by which harmonies could be further reduced to one of three essential types. The order of these is still widely accepted to determine musical syntax. The same theorist, however, generated minor harmony from a series of 'undertones' he believed he had derived mathematically. Alexander Rehding's classic monograph on the theorist begins with the affecting imagine of the scholar-musician listening late into the night for the undertones he was sure could produce at the piano.[18] Neither the overtone series, nor any fea-ture of the human hearing apparatus can serve as natural scientific basis for the rightness of minor harmony; and no undertones have yet been discovered. This puts harmonic theory at a serious disadvantage. If the explicandum is the apparent regularity of musical motion, then it can scarcely be denied that mode plays a key role in determining chordal vocabulary and applicable voice-leading conventions. Solving the problem of so-called 'harmonic dualism' by avoiding the puzzle of generation entirely, and instead locating its source in human artifice rather than nature does little more than describe the theory's limits.

3   Sensuous Human Practice

The critique Marx and Engels launched in the 1840s against their fellow Left Hegelians distinguished historical materialism from rival doctrines in terms of the theoretical priority it affords human productivity, or, in the terms of *The German Ideology*, sensuous practice. Evaluating music theories, one can find one's self torn between two criteria for judgement: 'rule and repertory'.[19] Eval-

---

17   Moreno 2004, 87.
18   Rehding 2003, 15.
19   The phrase is borrowed from Rehding, 2011.

uation can be based either in abstract principle, or on close checking against some repertoire or other. Both strategies, however, assume a detached, speculative position with respect to music making.

To be sure, classical harmonic theory was always intended to guide practice. Rameau's *Traité* begins as a scientific treatise and ends as a manual for the accompanist. Later in his career, he opened a private composition studio, and spent significant time working on a textbook for aspiring composers. While it remained unpublished at the end of his life, one of his students, Pietro Gianotti, revised and simplified the text, publishing it under the title *Guide for the Composer*.[20] Gianotti's preface makes clear what he deems the chief contribution of harmonic theory to musical practice to be. 'The true musician', he writes, 'prefers reason to caprice'.[21] He argues that musical instruction is in a sorry state insofar as the rules of composition are merely rules of thumb, an unsystematic collection of inherited prescriptions. Rameau's theoretical achievement made it possible to bring order to the diversity of views on musical construction. This diversity allowed each music master to propagate his own method without having to reconcile it with others. The student could therefore be caught between competing systems. Absent modern harmonic theory, musical rules represent engineering solutions to practical musical challenges. Like the rote operations that allowed the untutored builders of gothic cathedrals to erect immense arches without the aid of advanced mathematics or any knowledge of theoretical physics, the work of the musician was blindly mechanical.

While Rameau's system does offer the music student a streamlined conceptual architecture, reducing, as it does, vertical sonorities to only a handful of harmonic types, the action-guiding value of the science of chordal roots is not always obvious. Replacing engineering solutions with the results of deductive reasoning led some of Rameau's contemporaries to alter the very musical grammar his theoretical system was meant to codify. Jean-Paul Montagnier has shown that some strangely dissonant elaborations of cadential chordal progressions in solemn French music of the eighteenth century represent a misinterpretation of Rameau's theory.[22] Conflating sounded chords with fundamental harmonies, some composers chose to sound theoretically relevant, but always unsounded pitches, in the context of dissonant harmony, producing utterly novel sonorities. That Rameau's effort to simplify musical rules should have resulted in increased musical complexity is an irony that expresses the rift between harmonic theory and chordal practice.

---

20   Christensen 1993.

21   Gianotti 1759.

22   Montagnier, 2003.

A Marxist critique of harmonic ideology would aim at correcting for speculative distance by centring the conditions of musical production. In the first instance, this means abandoning the assumption that Rameau and his followers made genuine scientific discoveries, or indeed, that music theory can do the work of science at all. If the ontological status of harmonies cannot be determined, then space has been made for a successor theory to explain the apparent regularity of musical motion. Following Marx's lead, such an explanation would foreground the technical conditions of musical production. Harmonic theory arose inside the practice of thoroughbass music. As discussed in Chapter 6, the establishment and adoption of the continuous bass marked an efficiency breakthrough in the production of music. Thomas Christensen describes the way it directly informed harmonic theory, writing that thoroughbass –

> ... performers on guitars and theorboes tended to play and think of music in strongly vertical (harmonic) terms, and formulated their notation and pedagogy accordingly. Most of the realisations prescribed in the tutors [...] were strongly chordal, sometimes to the point of entirely discounting voice-leading considerations.[23]

To the extent that harmonies are thought to have been discovered rather than emitted in the process of making music under a certain dispensation of the productive forces, the relationship of thoroughbass to harmony is obscured. Carl Dahlhaus, for instance, writes that:

> ... the relationship of the practice of figured bass to the development of tonal harmony was an ambivalent one. On the one hand, figured bass encouraged the conception of the chord as the primary unit by designating vertical structures; the simultaneity was thought of as a tactile gesture rather than as the result of interwoven melodic parts. On the other hand, the experiencing of chords as based on roots, and the perceiving of the relationships between roots that build harmonic cohesion, were obstructed by the practice of figured bass: the emphasis on the actual basso continuo discouraged the awareness of the imaginary fundamental bass that was essential to the harmonic logic.[24]

Dahlhaus restricts the contribution of thoroughbass practice to the theory of harmony in order to make room for the discovery of harmonic logic. Even while

---

23   Christensen 1993, 48.
24   Dahlhaus 2001.

he leaves undecided the ontological status of the fundamental bass, harmony remains a feature of the world picked up on by 'awareness', rather than a mere mental component of a productive activity.

Some recent scholarship has demonstrated the potential of a practice-centred approach. Megan Long, for example, argues that chordal practice emerged in the late sixteenth century in light of conditions that selected for homophonic voice-leading.[25] She observes that the early market in printed music meant for domestic consumption included a great number of lighter pieces, little known or sung today. These set poetry with even lines and tight rhyme schemes, and the rhythmic outline of the whole often adopted the patterns of dance music. Relative simplicity and ease of use was essential to the genre. Naturally, this repertoire sold very well, and its patterns generated a vocabulary of simultaneities ready to be adapted to an instrument one is compelled to strum. The nature of these pieces also encouraged long-range expectations, given that the genre's conventions allowed the singer-listener the ability to predict musical events many bars ahead. A sense of harmonic tonality, then, arose in light of the habits of practice, a series of rules followed for their efficiency, but never consciously adopted by listeners or practitioners. The chordal vocabulary of what is sometimes called 'the common practice' arrived through an alienated force that demands similar solutions to similar engineering challenges, rather than through the unforced force of reason.

A critique of ideology not only identifies ideas that can be profitably abandoned in favour of properly scientific ones, but – perhaps just as importantly – serves to prevent the too-hasty dismissal of seemingly outmoded, non-scientific concepts. The Preface to *The German Ideology* relates the parable of the enlightened gentleman who is sure that gravity is just another scrap of clerical dogma. The man contends that if only the benighted victims of error could find it in themselves to leave this mental conception behind, they would evermore be safe from drowning. Should his too-clear-headed view have led him to jump into a lake with no plans to swim, we would be forced to conclude that this man would have been better served by a superstitious fear of water. Marx's early writings on religion make it clear that he is more concerned to illustrate the limits of simple-minded secularism than with mounting an attack on dogma. While 'the criticism of religion is the prerequisite of all criticism', religion is nevertheless 'the general theory of this world, its encyclopaedic compendium, its logic in popular form'. Far from falling unceremoniously into the dustbin of history at the moment the feudal economic structure dissolves, religion can be

---

25   Long 2020.

of some value to the revolutionist insofar as it generates emancipatory aspirations. As such, it is 'the expression of real suffering and a protest against real suffering, [...] the heart of a heartless world, and the soul of soulless conditions'.[26]

Following this lead, the materialist music theorist might replace theoretical with pragmatic concepts in an effort to reconstruct the tools of a music making practice on its own terms. Those terms need not be found in theoretical writing correspondent with a given style or period. Rather, one can look for conceptual determinacy embedded in the process of production itself. These are pragmatic, as opposed to theoretical, concepts insofar as they are evaluated in terms of their efficacy in the completion of tasks, rather than being measured against their representation of the world. These are rules of thumb, pre-scientific concepts that harmonic theory aimed to supplant by bringing speculative theory, like Adorno's stars, down to earth.[27]

A guiding thread in this effort is the growing literature on the patterned sequences and progressions that Robert Gjerdingen and others have found to structure music making in eighteenth century Europe.[28] A musician working in the prevailing musical language of court, church, and theatre would have at their disposal a series of prefab elements – sequences and cadences, in particular – that were rhythmically flexible and easily varied. The 'Romanesca', a leaping bass line paired with smoothly descending upper voices in thirds or sixths, is one such schema. It appears with startling frequency in the repertoire, despite its not appearing in primers on harmony from the period. The pattern is a balance of variety and connectivity, features that music learners at the time would have appreciated intuitively. The schema represents a practical solution to a voice leading problem, namely, the bass accompaniment of voices moving in parallel thirds or sixths. Interpreted as a chord progression, the Romanesca does not conform to a theory of chordal syntax derived from harmonic theory. Indeed, the progression itself is not best understood as expressing or representing harmonic motion at all. A music learner whose primary source of instruction in chordal use is one of the standard music theory textbooks taught in universities and conservatories today would have few resources for explaining the Romanesca, despite its musical virtues and frequent appearance.

The pattern presented no trouble for the eighteenth-century music learner, who absorbed a great deal of useful musical information by rote. This period saw the rise of the Neapolitan conservatory system, a network of trade schools

---

26   Marx 1992, 244.

27   Adorno 2001.

28   Gjerdingen 2007.

that set the international standard in musical training. In these institutions, children learned no speculative theory; instead, they were taught to improvise. The pedagogical approach does not come down to us through textbooks, but through a great many teaching compositions called 'partimenti' and 'solfeggi'. A partimento is a piece that consists in nothing but a bass line. A student trained to respond to the relevant pragmatic considerations would be expected to improvise upper voices over this written part, realising the full composition. A solfeggio is made up of a written melody over an unrealized bass line and serves as a singing exercise. The patterns that recur in these pieces developed the student's ear and familiarized them with best practices. As fully formed musician was one who had internalized a core set of music making habits.

Gjerdingen, who began his investigation into the patterns of the classical style from the perspective of music cognition, has competed a trajectory from theory to history in his most recent work, which is focused on the conservatory system.[29] That the work of music theory should lead the researcher to a detailed analysis of historical forms of training tracks an escape path from harmonic ideology. Gjerdingen goes as far as to stress the importance of social class in determining what kind of skills the musician acquired. Neither the traditional aristocracy nor the emergent bourgeoisie would have been incentivized to apprentice their children as musicians. In fact, the conservatory was originally intended to serve the poorest children, orphans, by providing them with a trade. There was nothing necessarily exalted in being a musician, despite the extreme refinement musical style had acquired. Both the nature of musical training and the style features it reinforced changed with changing social conditions. As industrial society ascended, the conservatory model gradually lost its social base.

A socialist materialist music theory explains the apparent regularity of voice leading with reference to productive efficiency, social history and the structure of institutions. In this way, it can make historically informed recommendations to the planners of the music making system in a post-capitalist order in which most productive enterprise is owned and operated in common. It would be both impossible and undesirable to attempt to re-establish something like the eighteenth-century training system in the twenty-first century. That said, understanding the precedent provides future planners with a model for which conditions are most conducive to the emergence of a common musical language in which most are able to freely improvise.

---

29   Gjerdingen 2020.

Bibliography

Adler, Guido 1904, *Richard Wagner: Vorlesungen gehalten an der Universität zu Wien*, Leipzig: Breitkopf und Härtel.

Adler, Guido 1911, *Stil in der Musik*, Leipzig: Breitkopf & Härtel.

Adler, Guido 1925, 'Internationalism in Music', translated by Theodore Baker, *The Musical Quarterly*, 11:281–300.

Adorno, Theodor 1973, *Negative Dialectics*, translated by E.B. Ashton, New York: Continuum.

Adorno, Theodor 1975, 'Culture Industry Reconsidered', *New German Critique* 6:12–19.

Adorno, Theodor, et al. 1976, *The Positivist Dispute in German Sociology*, translated by Glyn Adey and David Frisby, London: Heinemann.

Adorno, Theodor 1978, 'On the Social Situation of Music', translated by Wes Blomster, *Telos* 35:128–164.

Adorno, Theodor 1998 [1970], *Aesthetic Theory*, translated by Robert Hullot-Kentor, Minneapolis: University of Minnesota Press.

Adorno, Theodor 2001, *The Stars Down to Earth*, London: Routledge.

Adorno, Theodor and Max Horkheimer 2002 [1944], *Dialectic of Enlightenment: Philosophical Fragments*, edited by Gunzelin Schmid Noerr, translated by Edmund Jephcott, Stanford: Stanford University Press.

Anderson, Maynard 1966, 'On Teaching Musical Style', *Music Educators Journal*, 52:87–93.

Appelkvist, Hanne 2011, 'Form and Freedom: The Kantian Ethos of Musical Form', *Nordic Journal of Aesthetics*, 22:75–88.

Allen, Warren Dwight 1939, *Philosophies of Music History*, New York: American Book Company.

Arnold, F.T. 1965, *The Art of Accompaniment from a Thorough-Bass as Practiced in the XVIIth and XVIIIth Centuries*, Volume One, New York: Dover.

Attali, Jacques 1985, *Noise: The Political Economy of Music*, translated by Brian Massumi, Minneapolis: University of Minnesota Press.

Arvon, Henri 1970, *Marxist Esthetics*, translated by Helen Lane, Ithaca: Cornell University Press.

Bahti, Timothy 1987, 'Histories of the University: Kant and Humboldt' in *MLN* 102:437–460.

Bernstein, Eduard 1993 [1899], *The Preconditions of Socialism*, edited and translated by Henry Tudor, Cambridge: Cambridge University Press.

Bernstein, J.M. 2001, *Adorno: Disenchantment and Ethics*, Cambridge: Cambridge University Press.

Betz, Albrecht 1982, *Hanns Eisler: Political Musician*, translated by Bill Hopkins, Cambridge: Cambridge University Press.

Blake, David 2017, 'Musicological Omnivory in the Neoliberal University', *The Journal of Musicology* 34:319–353.

Bloch, Ernst 2000 [1918], *The Spirit of Utopia*, Stanford: Stanford University Press.

Bohlman, Philip 1993, 'Musicology as a Political Act', *The Journal of Musicology*, 11:411–436.

Böhm-Bawerk, Eugen von 1996, *Karl Marx and the Close of His System*, edited by Paul Sweezy, New York: Augustus Kelly.

Bogdanov, Alexander 2015 [1913], *The Philosophy of Living Experience*, translated by David G. Rowley, Leiden: Brill.

Bosworth Powers, David 1995, 'Johann Nikolaus Forkel's Philosophy of Music in the *Einleitung* to Volume One of his *Allgemeine Geschichte der Musik* (1788): A Translation and Commentary with a Glossary of Eighteenth-Century Terms', PhD Dissertation, University of North Carolina, Chapel Hill.

Brandenberger, David and Mikhail Zelenov (eds.) 2019, *Stalin's Master Narrative: A Critical Edition of the* History of the Communist Party of the Soviet Union (Bolsheviks): Short Course, New Haven: Yale University Press.

Brandom, Robert 2006, 'Kantian Lessons about Mind, Meaning, and Rationality', *Philosophical Topics*, 1:1–20.

Breuer, Benjamin 2011, 'The Birth of Musicology from the Spirit of Evolution: Ernst Haeckel's *Entwicklungslehre* as Central Component of Guido Adler's Methodology', PhD Dissertation, University of Pittsburgh.

Brilmayer, Benedikt and Casey Mongoven 2012, *Johann David Heinichen's* Gründliche Anweisung *(1711): Comprehensive Introduction on Basso Continuo with Historical Biographies*, Sheffield, MA: Pendragon Press.

Brook, Barry Edward Downes, and Sherman van Solkema (eds.) 1972, *Perspectives in Musicology: The Inaugural Lectures of the Ph.D. Program in Music at the City University of New York*, New York: W.W. Norton.

Broude, Ronald 2020, 'To Sing Upon the Book: Oral and Written Counterpoint in Early Modern Europe', *Textual Cultures*, 13:75–105.

Buckley, Ann 2000, 'Music and Musicians in Medieval Irish Society', *Early Music*, 28:165–190.

Bukharin, Nikolai 1925, *Historical Materialism: A System of Sociology*, Moscow: International Publishers.

Bukharin, Nikolai and E. Preobrazhensky 1969, *The ABC of Communism*, translated by Eden and Cedar Paul, New York: Penguin.

Busse Berger, Anna Maria 2005, *Medieval Music and the Art of Memory*, Berkeley: University of California Press.

Carlton, Richard A. 2006, 'Changes in Status and Role-Play: The Musician and the End of the Eighteenth Century', *International Review of the Aesthetics and Sociology of Music* 37:3–16.

Carter, Tim and Richard A. Goldthwaite 2013, *Orpheus in the Marketplace: Jacopo Peri and the Economy of Late Renaissance Florence*, Cambridge: Harvard University Press.

Carver, Terrell 2010, 'The German Ideology Never Took Place', *History of Political Thought* 31:107–127.

Christensen, Thomas 1993, *Rameau and Musical Thought in the Enlightenment*, Cambridge: Cambridge University Press.

Citron, Marcia 1990, 'Gender, Performance and the Musical Canon', *The Journal of Musicology*, 8:102–117.

Clawson, Mary Ann 1985, 'Fraternal Orders and Class Formation in the Nineteenth-Century United States', *Comparative Studies in Society and History* 27:672–695.

Cohen, G.A. 1978, *Karl Marx's Theory of History: A Defence*, Princeton, NJ: Princeton University Press.

Countryman, Vern 1948, 'The Organized Musicians: I', *The University of Chicago Law Review*, 16:56–85.

Crocker, Richard 1966, *A History of Musical Style*, New York: McGraw-Hill.

Dahlhaus, Carl 1972, *Analysis and Value Judgement*, London: Pendragon Press.

Dahlhaus, Carl 1983, *Foundations of Music History*, translated by J.B. Robinson, Cambridge: Cambridge University Press.

Dahlhaus, Carl 2001, 'Harmony', *Grove Music Online*.

Dobb, Maurice 1946, *Studies in the Development of Capitalism*, London: Routledge.

Eagleton, Terry 2011, *Why Marx Was Right*, New Haven: Yale University Press.

Edmunds, Neil 2000, *The Soviet Proletarian Music Movement*, Bern: Peter Lang.

Eisler, Hanns 1978, *A Rebel in Music: Selected Writings*, edited by Manfred Grabs, London: Kahn & Averill.

Engels, Friedrich 1972, 'Realism and Didacticism', in *Marxism and Art: Writings in Aesthetics and Criticism*, edited by Barel Lang and Forrest Williams, New York: David McKay.

Forkel, Johann Nikolaus 1777, *Uber die Theorie der Musik*, Göttingen: Verlag der Wittwe Bandenhöck.

Freyenhagen, Fabian 2014, 'Adorno's Politics: Theory and Praxis in Germany's 1960s', *Philosophy and Social Criticism* 40:867–893.

Fuchs, Christian 2020. *Communication and Capitalism: A Critical Theory*, London: University of Westminster Press.

Gianotti, Pietro 1759, *Le Guide du Compositeur*, Paris: Durand.

Gjerdingen, Robert 2007, *Music in the Galant Style*, Oxford: Oxford University Press.

Gjerdingen, Robert 2020, *Child Composers in the Old Conservatories: How Orphans Became Elite Musicians*, Oxford: Oxford University Press.

Goehr, Lydia 1992, *The Imaginary Museum of Musical Works: An Essay in the Philosophy of Music*, Oxford: Oxford University Press.

Glixon, Beth L. and Jonathan E. Glixon 2006, *Inventing the Business of Opera: The Impresario and His World in Seventeenth-Century Venice*, Oxford: Oxford University Press.

Glixon, Jonathan 1983, 'A Musicians' Union in Sixteenth-Century Venice', *Journal of the American Musicological Society*, 36:392–421.

Gorky, Maxim 1977, 'Soviet Literature', in *Soviet Writers' Congress 1934: The Debate on Socialist Realism and Modernism in the Soviet Union*, London: Lawrence and Wishart.

Grossman, Henryk 1992, *The Law of Accumulation and Breakdown of the Capitalist System*, translated by Jairus Banaji, London: Pluto Press.

Grout, Donald and Claude Palisca 1988, *A History of Western Music*, 4th edition, New York: W.W. Norton.

Habermas, Jürgen 1987 [1968], *Knowledge and Human Interests*, translated by Jeremy J. Shapiro, Cambridge, UK: Polity Press.

Haggh, Barbara 1989, 'Itinerancy to Residency: Professional Careers and Performance Practices in 15th-Century Sacred Music', *Early Music*, 17:359–366.

Hanslick, Eduard 1869, *Geschichte des Concertwesens in Wien*, Vienna: W. Braumüller.

Hanslick, Eduard 1963, *Music Criticisms 1848–99*, translated by Henry Pleasants, New York: Penguin Books.

Hanslick, Eduard 2018 [1854], *Eduard Hanslick's* On The Musically Beautiful: *A New Translation*, edited and translated by Lee Rothfarb and Christoph Landerer, Oxford: Oxford University Press.

Harley, C.K. and N.F.R. Crafts 1995, 'Cotton Textiles and Industrial Output Growth during the Industrial Revolution', *The Economic History Review*, 48:134–144.

Harvey, David 2018, *A Companion to Marx's* Capital: *The Complete Edition*, London: Verso.

Haydon, Glen 1963, 'Music Theory and Music History', *Journal of Music Theory*, 7:249–255.

Hegel, G.W.F. 2018 [1807], *The Phenomenology of Spirit*, translated by Terry Pinkard, Cambridge: Cambridge University Press.

Hegel, G.W.F. 2019 [1807], *The Phenomenology of Spirit*, translated by Peter Fuss and John Dobbins, Notre Dame: University of Notre Dame Press.

Heinrich, Michael 2012, *An Introduction to the three Volumes of Karl Marx's* Capital, translated by Alex Locasio, New York: Monthly Review Press.

Heller, Agnes 1978, 'The Positivism Dispute as a Turning Point in German Post-War Theory', *New German Critique*, 15:49–56.

Heller, Henry 2016, *The Capitalist University: The Transformations of Higher Education in the United States, 1945–2016*, New York: Pluto Press.

Helmholtz, Hermann von 1954 [1863], *On the Sensation of Tone*, Mineola, NY: Dover Publications.

Henrich, Dieter 1992, *Aesthetic Judgment and the Moral Image of the World: Studies in Kant*, Sanford: Stanford University Press.

Hepokoski, James 1991, 'The Dahlhaus Project and Its Extra-Musicological Sources', *19th-Century Music* 14:221–246.

Hilferding, Rudolf 1981 [1919], *Finance Capital*, translated by Morris Watnick and Sam Gordon, London: Routledge.

Höflechner, Walter 2017, 'The Thunian Reforms in the Context of the Development of the Science in Austria', in Christof Aichner and Brigitte Mazohl (eds.), *The Thun-Hohenstein University Reforms 1849–1860: Conception, Implementation, Aftermath*, Vienna: Böhlau Verlag.

Hubbard, Preston J. 1985, 'Synchronized Sound and Movie-House Musicians, 1926–29', *American Music*, 3:429–441.

Hullot-Kentor, Robert 2008, 'The Exact Sense in Which the Culture Industry No Longer Exists', *Cultural Critique* 70:137–157.

Huyssen, Andreas 1989, 'Adorno in Reverse: From Hollywood to Richard Wagner', *New German Critique* 29:8–38.

James, Robin 2010, *The Conjectural Body: Gender, Race, and the Philosophy of Music*, Lanham: Lexington Books.

Jameson, Fredric 2009, *Valences of the Dialectic*, London: Verso.

Jeppesen, Knud 1970, *The Style of Palestrina and the Dissonance*, Toronto: Dover Publications.

Johnston, William 1967, 'Karl Marx's Verse of 1836–1837 as a Foreshadowing of his Early Philosophy', *Journal of the History of Ideas*, 28:259–268.

Kant, Immanuel 1979, *The Conflict of the Faculties*, translated by Mary Gregor, New York: Abaris Books.

Karnes, Kevin 2008, *Music, Criticism, and the Challenge of History: Shaping Modern Musical Thought in Late Nineteenth Century Vienna*, Oxford: Oxford University Press.

Kautsky, Karl 1925, *Foundations of Christianity: A Study in Christian Origins*, New York: International Publishers.

Kautsky, Karl 1983, *Karl Kautsky: Selected Political Writings*, edited and translated by Patrick Goode, London: Macmillan Press.

Kerman, Joseph 1965, 'A Profile for American Musicology', *Journal of the American Musicological Society* 18:61–69.

Kerman, Joseph 1980, 'How We Got into Analysis and How to Get Out', *Critical Inquiry* 7:311–331.

Kerman, Joseph 1986, *Contemplating Music*, Cambridge: Harvard University Press.

Kiesewetter, R.G. 1848, *History of the Modern Music of Western Europe*, London: T.C. Newby.

Kliman, Andrew 2007, *Reclaiming Marx's Capital: A Refutation of the Myth of Inconsistency*, Lanham, MD: Lexington Books.

Kliman, Andrew 2011, *The Failure of Capitalist Production: Underlying Causes of the Great Recession*, London: Pluto.

Knepler, Georg 1977, *Geschichte als Weg zum Musikverständnis*, Berlin: Reclam.

Knepler, Georg 1994, *Wolfgang Amadé Mozart*, translated by J. Bradford Robinson, Cambridge: Cambridge University Press.

Krader, Barbara 1990. 'Recent Achievements in Soviet Ethnomusicology, with Remarks on Russian Terminology', *Yearbook for Traditional Music* 22:1–16.

Kraft, James P. 1996, *Stage to Studio: Musicians and the Sound Revolution, 1890–1950*, Baltimore: Johns Hopkins University Press.

Kursell, Julia 2015, 'A Third Note: Helmholtz, Palestrina, and the Early History of Musicology', *Isis* 106:353–366.

Labriola, Antonio 1908 [1895], *Essays on the Materialistic Conception of History*, Chicago: Charles Kerr and Company.

Lang, Paul Henry 1941, *Music in Western Civilisation*, New York: Norton.

Laing, Dave 1978, *The Marxist Theory of Art*, Sussex: The Harvester Press.

Larraín, Jorge 1979, *The Concept of Ideology*, Athens, GA: University of Georgia Press.

Larson, Steven 1994, 'Another Look at Schenker's 'Counterpoint', *Indiana Theory Review* 15:44.

Lenin, Vladimir 1971 [1905], 'Party Organisation and Party Literature', in *Socialist Realism in Literature and Art: A Collection of Articles*, Moscow: Progress Publishers.

Lenin, Vladimir 1971 [1913], 'The Development of Workers' Choirs in Germany', in *Collected Works*, Volume 36, Moscow: Progress Publishers.

Lifshitz, Mikhail 2018 [1968], *The Crisis of Ugliness: From Cubism to Pop-Art*, translated by David Riff, Chicago: Haymarket.

Lindley, Mark 2010, 'Marx and Engels on Music', *Monthly Review Online*, available at https://mronline.org/2010/08/18/marx-and-engels-on-music/.

Lloyd, Llewelyn 1939, 'Helmholtz and the Musical Ear', *The Musical Quarterly* 25:167–175.

Long, Megan Kees 2020, *Hearing Homophony: Tonal Expectation at the Turn of the Seventeenth Century*, Oxford: Oxford University Press.

Lukács, Georg 1969, 'Die Sickingendebatte zwischen Marx, Engels und Lassalle', in Georg Lukács, *Probleme der Ästhetik*, Darmstadt: Lichterhand.

Lukács, Georg 1970, 'The Old Culture and the New Culture', *Telos* 5:21–30.

Lukács, György 1971, 'Béla Bartók: On the 25th Anniversary of his Death', *The Hungarian Quarterly*, 41:42–55.

Lukács, Georg 1972, *History and Class Consciousness: Studies in Marxist Dialectics*, translated by Rodney Livingstone, Cambridge: MIT Press.

Lukács, Georg 1963, *Die Eigenart des Ästhetischen*, Volume 2, Munich: Lichterhand.

Lukács, Georg 1981, *Essays on Realism*, translated by David Fernbach, Cambridge: MIT Press.

Luxemburg, Rosa 2004 [1900], 'Social Reform or Revolution', in Peter Hudis and Kevin Anderson (eds.), *The Rosa Luxemburg Reader*, New York: Monthly Review Press.

Mally, Lynn 1990, *The Proletkult Movement in Revolutionary Russia*, Berkeley: University of California Press.

Maróthy, János 1974, *Music and the Bourgeois, Music and the Proletarian*, translated by Eva Róna, Budapest: Akademémiai Kiadó.

Marramao, Giacomo 1975, 'Political Economy and Critical Theory', *Telos* 24:56–80.

Martherne, Samantha 2014, 'Kant's Expressive Theory of Music', *The Journal of Aesthetics and Art Criticism*, 72:129–145.

Marx, Karl 1964, *Selected Writings in Sociology and Social Philosophy*, edited and translated by T.B. Bottomore, New York: McGraw Hill.

Marx, Karl 1973 [1857–58], *Grundrisse: Foundations of the Critique of Political Economy (Rough Draft)*, translated by Martin Nicolaus, New York: Penguin Books.

Marx, Karl 1976 [1867], *Capital: A Critique of Political Economy*, translated by Ben Fowkes, New York: Penguin.

Marx, Karl 1983 [1881], *The Mathematical Manuscripts of Karl Marx*, translated by C. Aronson and M. Meo, London: New Park Publications.

Marx, Karl 1988 [1844], *Economic and Philosophic Manuscripts*, translated by Martin Milligan, New York: Prometheus Books.

Marx, Karl 1992, *Early Writings*, translated by Rodney Livingstone and Gregor Benton, New York: Penguin.

Mathiesen, Thomas 1975, 'An Annotated Translation of Euclid's 'Division of the Monochord'', *Journal of Music Theory*, 19:236–258.

Mattick, Paul 2011, *Business as Usual: The Economic Crisis and the Failure of Capitalism*, London: Reaktion Books.

McClary, Susan 2000, *Conventional Wisdom: The Content of Musical Form*, Berkeley: University of California Press.

Gordon McQuere, Gordon (ed.) 1983. *Russian Theoretical Thought in Music*, Rochester, NY: University of Rochester Press.

McGee, Timothy 1995, 'The Fall of the Noble Minstrel: The Sixteenth-Century Minstrel in a Musical Context', *Medieval and Renaissance Drama in England*, 7:98–120.

Menke, Christoph 1998, *The Sovereignty of Art: Aesthetic Negativity in Adorno and Derrida*, translated by Neil Solomon, Cambridge: MIT Press.

Merleau-Ponty, Maurice 1973, *Adventures of the Dialectic*, translated by Joseph Bien, Evanston: Northwestern University Press.

Miller Harris, Sarah 2016, *The CIA and the Congress for Cultural Freedom in the Early Cold War: The Limits of Making Common Cause*, London: Routledge.

Montagnier, Jean-Paul 2003, 'Heavenly Dissonances: The Cadential Six-Four Chord in French Grant Motets and Rameau's Theory of Accord par Supposition', *Journal of Music Theory* 47:305–323.

Moore, Allan 2001, 'Categorical Conventions in Music Discourse: Style and Genre', *Music & Letters*, 82:432–442.

Moore, Julia 1991, 'Review: *Music Matters: The Performer and the American Federation of Musicians* by George Seltzer Metuchen', *Notes*, 48:135–138.

Moreno, Jairo 2004, *Musical Representations, Subjects, and Objects: The Construction of Musical Thought in Zarlino, Descartes, Rameau, and Weber*, Bloomington, IN: Indiana University Press.

Moseley, Fred 2017, *Money and Totality: A Macro-Monetary Interpretation of Marx's Logic in* Capital *and the End of the 'Transformation Problem'*, Chicago: Haymarket.

Mugglestone, Erica 1981, 'Guido Adler's 'The Scope, Method and Aim of Musicology': An English Translation with an Historic-Analytical Commentary', *Yearbook for Traditional Music*, 13:1–21.

Mundy, Rachel 2014, 'Evolutionary Categories and Musical Style from Adler to America', *Journal of the American Musicological Society*, 67:735–768.

Nytch, Jeffrey 2018, *The Entrepreneurial Muse: Imagining Your Career in Classical Music*, Oxford: Oxford University Press.

Okiji, Fumi 2008, *Jazz as Critique: Adorno and Black Expression Revisited*, Stanford: Stanford University Press.

Owens, Jessie Ann 1997, *Composers at Work: The Craft of Musical Composition, 1450–1600*, Oxford: Oxford University Press.

Parenti, Michael 1997, *Blackshirts and Reds: Rational Fascism and the Overthrow of Communism*, San Francisco: City Lights Books.

Peterson, Marina 2013, 'Sound Work: Music as Labor and the 1940s Recording Bans of the American Federation of Musicians', *Anthropological Quarterly*, 86:791–823.

Postone, Moishe and Barbara Brick 1982, 'Critical Pessimism and the Limits of Traditional Marxism', *Theory and Society*, 11:617–658.

Postone, Moishe 1993, *Time, Labor, and Social Domination: A Reinterpretation of Marx's Critical Theory*, Cambridge: Cambridge University Press.

Potter, Pamela 1998, *Most German of the Arts: Musicology and Society from the Weimar Republic to the End of the Third Reich*, New Haven: Yale University Press.

Rameau, Jean-Philippe 1971 [1722], *Treatise on Harmony*, translated by Philip Gossett, Mineola, NY: Dover Publications.

Raynor, Henry and Robert Stevens 1934, 'Fascism and the Ministry of Fine Arts', *The Musical Times*, 75:737–738.

Raynor, Henry 1978, *A Social History of Music from the Middle Ages to Beethoven*, New York: Taplinger.

Rehding, Alexander 2003, *Hugo Riemann and the Birth of Modern Musical Thought*, Cambridge: Cambridge University Press.

Rehding, Alexander 2011, 'Tonality Between Rule and Repertory; Or, Riemann's Functions – Beethoven's Function', *Music Theory Spectrum* 33:109–123.

Ritchey, Marianna 2019, *Composing Capital: Classical Music in the Neoliberal Era*, Chicago: University of Chicago Press.

Rosand, Ellen 1991, *Opera in Seventeenth-Century Venice: The Creation of a Genre*. Berkeley: University of California Press.

Rosdolsky, Roman 1977, *The Making of Marx's 'Capital'*, translated by Pete Burgess, London: Pluto Press.

Rosenthal, Carl 1985–86, 'Reminiscences of Guido Adler (1855–1941)', *Musica Judaica*, 8:13–22.

Ross, Dorothy 1988, 'On the Misunderstanding of Ranke and the Origins of the Historical Profession in America', *Syracuse Scholar*, 9:31–41.

Rubin, I.I. 2008 [1923], *Essays on Marx's Theory of Value*, translated by Milos Samardzija and Fredy Perlman, Delhi: Aakar Books.

Schubert, Peter 2020, '*Contrapunto Fugato*: A First Step Toward Composing in the Mind', *Music Theory Spectrum*, 42:260–279.

Semper, Gottfried 2004 [1860], *Style in the Technical and Tectonic Arts, Or, Practical Aesthetics*, Los Angeles: Getty Research Institute.

Seltzer, George 1989, *Music Matters: The Performer and the American Federation of Musicians*, Metuchen NJ: Scarecrow Press.

Shaikh, Anwar 2016, *Capitalism: Competition, Conflict, Crises*, Oxford: Oxford University Press.

Shreffler, Anne 2003, 'Berlin Walls: Dahlhaus, Knepler, and the Ideologies of Music History', *The Journal of Musicology*, 20:498–525.

Strohm, Reinhard 1993, *The Rise of European Music 1380–1500*, Cambridge: Cambridge University Press.

Strunk, Oliver (ed.) 1950, *Source Readings in Music History from Classical Antiquity Through the Romantic Era*, New York: Norton.

Taruskin, Richard 2010, *Oxford History of Western Music, Volume 1: From the Earliest Notations to the Sixteenth Century*, Oxford: Oxford University Press.

Taylor, Charles 1977, *Hegel*, Cambridge: Cambridge University Press.

Toews, John 1985, *Hegelianism: The Path Toward Dialectical Humanism*, Cambridge: University of Cambridge Press.

Toews, John 1993, 'Transformations of Hegelianism, 1805–1846', in *The Cambridge Companion to Hegel*, Cambridge: Cambridge University Press.

Tomlinson, Gary 2013, 'Evolutionary Studies in the Humanities: The Case of Music', *Critical Inquiry*, 39:647–675.

Treitler, Leo 1989, 'Review: The Power of Positivist Thinking', *Journal of the American Musicological Society*, 42:375–402.

Tull, Robert James 1976. *B.V. Asaf'ev's* Musical Form as Process: *Translation and Commentary*, Ph.D. Dissertation, Ohio State University.

Varoufakis, Yanis 2015, 'How I Became an Erratic Marxist', *The Guardian*, available at https://www.theguardian.com/news/2015/feb/18/yanis-varoufakis-how-i-became-an-erratic-marxist.

Wagner, Richard 1993, *The Art-Work of the Future and Other Works*, translated by William Ashton Ellis, Lincoln: University of Nebraska Press.

Wagner Oettinger, Rebecca 2004, 'Berg v. Gerlach: Printing and Lasso's Imperial Privilege of 1582', *Fontes Artis Musicae*, 51:111–134.

Wallin, Nils Björn Merker, and Steven Brown 2000, 'An Introduction to Evolutionary Musicology', in *The Origin of Music*, edited by Wallin, Merker and Brown, Cambridge MA: MIT Press.

Weber, William (ed.) 2004, *The Musician as Entrepreneur, 1700–1914: Managers, Charlatans, and Idealists*, Bloomington: Indiana University Press.

Wegman, Rob 1996, 'From Maker to Composer', *Journal of the American Musicological Society*, 49:409–479.

Wegman, Rob 2005, *The Crisis of Music in Early Modern Europe*, New York: Routledge.

Wilfing, Alexander 2018, 'Hanslick, Kant, and the Origins of *Vom Musikalisch-Schönen*', *Musicologica Austriaca: Journal for Austrian Music Studies*.

Williamson, John and Martin Cloonan 2016, *Players' Work Time: A History of the British Musicians' Union, 1893–2013*, Manchester, UK: Manchester University Press.

Yoshida, Hiroshi 2001, 'Eduard Hanslick and the Idea of 'Public' in Music Culture: Towards a Socio-Political Context of Formalistic Aesthetics', *International Review of the Aesthetics and Sociology of Music*, 32:179–199.

Zemon Davis, Natalie 1966, 'A Trade Union in Sixteenth-Century France', *The Economic History Review*, 19:48–69.

Zguta, Russell 1972, 'Skomorokhi: The Russian Minstrel-Entertainers', *Slavic Review*, 31:297–313.

Zhdanov, Andrei 1950, *Essays on Literature, Philosophy and Music*, New York: International Publishers.

Žižek, Slavoj 1989, *The Sublime Object of Ideology*, London: Verso Books.

Zuckert, Rachel 2010, *Kant on Beauty and Biology: An Interpretation of the Critique of Judgment*, Cambridge: Cambridge University Press.

Index

www.ingramcontent.com/pod-product-compliance
Lightning Source LLC
Chambersburg PA
CBHW061800120626
46550CB00005B/2066